THe PATH to KiNDNeSS

POEMS OF CONNECTION AND JOY

Edited by
James Crews

Foreword by
Danusha Laméris

Storey Publishing

The mission of Storey Publishing is to serve our customers by publishing practical information that encourages personal independence in harmony with the environment.

Edited by Liz Bevilacqua
Art direction and book design by Alethea Morrison
Text production by Slavica A. Walzl
Cover art and illustrations by © Dinara Mirtalipova

Storey books are available at special discounts when purchased in bulk for premiums and sales promotions as well as for fund-raising or educational use. Special editions or book excerpts can also be created to specification. For details, please call 800-827-8673, or send an email to sales@storey.com.

Storey Publishing
210 MASS MoCA Way
North Adams, MA 01247
storey.com

Printed in the United States by Lakeside Book Company
10 9 8 7 6 5 4 3 2 1

Library of Congress Cataloging-in-Publication Data on file

Your legacy is every life you touch.
Maya Angelou

CONTENTS

FOREWORD

Most of us spend a lot of time waiting for the right moment, by which I mean the moment when everything is as we want it to be: the laundry done, the faucet fixed, the kids all getting along with each other. We wait for it to rain, or for it to stop raining. For the pandemic to be over. For a baby to be born, or for the kids to leave the house. Wait until we get the promotion, the car, the partner. The conditions we place on our experience of life are endless.

And when I'm struck by a moment of sanity, I notice those conditions falling away, if only for an instant. The house is a mess, and yet, here I am, as I was earlier today, accepting a rose from a woman I don't even know, who, on the small country road where I walk with my husband, ran after me to extend her hand and offer a flower the most brilliant shades of pink and apricot, the petals ruffled like petticoats. "Here!" she said. "For you!" And I don't know what was more beautiful: the rose, or the effort she made to deliver it. For the whole walk, it glowed, a presence, between us.

Meanwhile, wars waged on, the hospital wards remained full, many went to bed hungry. How do we live in the gap between the hoped-for and the real?

We want the world to be less broken. Ourselves to be less broken. To love an unbroken person. But here we are. So many days, it's difficult to carry on. The simple, mammalian pleasure of touch can be the anchor we need. Or witnessing a beloved engaged in an everyday task—like washing dishes, or braiding a child's hair—and there it is, the breath of the sacred.

What we really want to know is, "Am I welcome here? Am I part of the tribe? Do I have a place?" And so, when a stranger offers a flower, it seems possible. Possible that we are meant to be exactly where—and who—we are. That we are meant.

The most memorable moments of my life are often the smallest. Not my college graduation (a blur), but the moment a little girl took the ends of my scarf when I was walking through a crowd at the farmer's market, and began to twirl, inviting me into an impromptu *pas de deux*. It seemed no one else saw it, and so it felt as if we'd stepped outside of time.

Kindness is not sugar, but salt. A dash of it gives the whole dish flavor. I want to keep remembering, to keep living into these moments and the worlds they contain. To know they are where the world I want to live in is made. That it is made right here, in the heart of the broken, the ordinary. These poems remind me. These voices give shape to that world. They show a way.

Danusha Laméris

THE PRACTICE OF
CONNECTION

When my husband, Brad, was nineteen years old, he joined the military, hoping to follow in the footsteps of his uncle and grandfather. During his first few weeks at the assigned Air Force base, however, he fell into a deep depression. After a few sessions with the on-base psychologist, he finally realized he was gay and came out. "You know what this means," the psychologist said. It meant that under the Don't Ask, Don't Tell policy, he was soon discharged from the military and sent home. I can only imagine the shame that followed him to the small town in Vermont where he grew up, and where he told no one for years the real reason he'd left the Air Force.

Brad first shared this story with me not long after we moved in together. "Suicide was a daily option," he said. The idea that this gentle farmer, who uplifts everyone he meets and cares so much for the land, might have ended his life still seems inconceivable to me. Yet what kept him pushing through those dark days, he says, were the small kindnesses offered by neighbors, friends, and customers at the organic farm where he began to work. He would be out for a run or walk, certain that this would be the day he could bear his secret no longer, and someone passing by in their pickup truck would wave, or a friend of the family would stop to ask how he was doing. The weight of his shame became lighter, and he knew he could keep going for another day.

As a lifelong city dweller, I struggled at first with receiving all the caring attention from friends and family in our small community. But after Brad shared his story with me, and then with the whole state of Vermont during his campaign for the US Senate, I soon saw how the daily kindnesses were saving me as well. I felt it when my mother-in-law called if she saw an unfamiliar car in our driveway; when our neighbor Christy would leave mason jars of fresh-pressed apple cider on our side porch; or when my father-in-law would wake early after a nor'easter to plow our driveway. I began to see too that we can create a beloved community like this no matter where we live.

Many of us have faced times when life felt impossible to bear—until a friend texted, or the barista at our favorite coffee shop started chatting with us. Because the sparks of connections like this last for just a few minutes, we might lose heart, believing that what little we can give to each other will have no lasting effect on a world that feels so broken and divided. But my hope is that, as you read through the poems gathered here, you will see kindness not just as a spontaneous act that happens on its own, but as a *practice* of noticing and naming the many moments of tenderness we witness, give, and receive throughout our days. Over the past year, as I shared these poems with students, family, and friends, I felt profoundly moved by the goodness they seem to prove is our basic human nature. It has become a daily, conscious ritual for me to hold on to as many of my own small kindnesses as possible in what social psychologist Barbara Fredrickson calls "moments of positive resonance."

These poems retrained me to seek out and find connection at a time when so many of us have grown more isolated. Sometimes a simple hello from someone I passed on the trail in the park or a glimmer in the eyes of a grocery-store cashier was enough to restore my faith in humanity for another day. I began to find ways to be kinder to the people in my own life, too, welcoming the task of helping my elderly mother order groceries online, or sending care packages to friends I hadn't seen in months. By showing us all the ways we can still practice being together, these poems encourage us to capture and hold on to the moments that matter the most to us in life. Many of the poems included here also model for us the ways that we might let ourselves surrender more fully to joy, especially in service of self-care. In "Ode," Zoe Higgins uncovers the pleasure of leaving "everything undone" and relieving herself of the constant pressure of the to-do list. And in "Before I gained all this weight," Molly Fisk shares the desire to go back and shake the girl she once was, awakening her to all the beauty she couldn't see around her because of shame and fear.

Because a poem contains just a dose of the author's experience, including the sorrows, pleasures, and struggles all at the same time, it offers us the truest expression of the human condition. If we let it, each poem here can become an invitation to step deeper into our own lives and relationships with others, too. We might read a poem like Christine Kitano's "For the Korean Grandmother on Sunset Boulevard" and remember that we can find pleasure and kinship even in the simplest observation of a stranger to whom we never speak. Or we might take in the motherly sacrifice at the heart of Ada Limón's "The Raincoat" and Faith Shearin's "My Mother's Van," and recall the sacrifices our own loved ones made for us, or that we made for others. These poems also urge us toward a deeper relationship with the natural world so that we notice, as January Gill O'Neil does in "Elation," the way a grove of trees will "claim this space as their own, making the most of what's given them," just like we do. I encourage you to use these poems, Reflective Pauses, and Discussion Questions at the end of the book as companions on your own path. Let a poem bring some memory to the surface or follow the call of an opening line or image to some truth of your own, whether you write it down or share it with someone you trust.

Poetry is an ideal tool in times of uncertainty and change in our lives because it grounds us in the now, opening our hearts and minds to the worlds outside and within. Please feel free to share the poems that move you with family and friends, allowing these deeply felt pieces to bring us all closer together until we see, as Dr. Martin Luther King Jr. put it so well, that we are all "caught in an inescapable network of mutuality, tied in a single garment of destiny." Perhaps that's why, when my husband and I take our daily walks on the roads around our house, we make a point of waving and smiling at every person and every car we pass. We both know all too well that a simple gesture of welcome might change someone's day and might even save their life.

James Crews

Danusha Laméris

SMALL KINDNESSES

I've been thinking about the way, when you walk
down a crowded aisle, people pull in their legs
to let you by. Or how strangers still say "bless you"
when someone sneezes, a leftover
from the Bubonic plague. "Don't die," we are saying.
And sometimes, when you spill lemons
from your grocery bag, someone else will help you
pick them up. Mostly, we don't want to harm each other.
We want to be handed our cup of coffee hot,
and to say thank you to the person handing it. To smile
at them and for them to smile back. For the waitress
to call us honey when she sets down the bowl of clam
    chowder,
and for the driver in the red pick-up truck to let us pass.
We have so little of each other, now. So far
from tribe and fire. Only these brief moments of exchange.
What if they are the true dwelling of the holy, these
fleeting temples we make together when we say, "Here,
have my seat," "Go ahead—you first," "I like your hat."

Naomi Shihab Nye

RED BROCADE

The Arabs used to say,
When a stranger appears at your door,
feed him for three days
before asking who he is,
where he's come from,
where he's headed.
That way, he'll have strength
enough to answer.
Or, by then you'll be
such good friends
you don't care.

Let's go back to that.
Rice? Pine nuts?
Here, take the red brocade pillow.
My child will serve water
to your horse.

No, I was not busy when you came!
I was not preparing to be busy.
That's the armor everyone put on
to pretend they had a purpose
in the world.

I refuse to be claimed.
Your plate is waiting.
We will snip fresh mint
into your tea.

Shari Altman

WORRY STONE FOR MY GRANDFATHER

You let me cut the mint,
put me in charge of taming the kittens.
We picked tomatoes and beans
in a bushel basket, collected
water from the healing springs.
For years you saved me with action,
the beauty and relief of work.

When you became sick,
who knows how our thoughts collided?

A worry stone passed from young to old,
smoothed down by a thumbprint.
I had nothing else to give.
When you gave it back to me,
I did not expect it, found it hard
to witness your acceptance.

On the day you died
I brought you a poinsettia,
the same red as your favorite sweater
that lives in my closet now.
I still believed
in invincibility.

My limp wrist, the tilt
of the pot brushing the ground.

Rosemerry Wahtola Trommer

KINDNESS

Consider the tulip,
how long ago
someone's hands planted a bulb
and gave to this place
a living scrap of beauty,
how it rises every spring
out of the same soil,
which is, of course,
not at all the same soil,
but new.

Consider the six red petals,
the yellow at the center,
the soft green rubber of the stem,
how it bows to the world.
How, the longer you sit beside the tulip,
the more you want to bow, too.

It is this way with kindness:
someone plants in someone else
a bit of beauty—
a kind word, perhaps, or a touch,
the gift of their time or their smile.
And years later, in that inner soil,
that beauty emerges again,
pushing aside the dead leaves,
insisting on loveliness,

a celebration of the one who planted it,
the one who perceives it, and
the fertile place where it has grown.

The Soil That Is You

Our bodies and minds often hold on to memories of past wrongs and ways that others have harmed us more strongly than anything else. This makes sense; after all, we don't want to be hurt again. Yet we sometimes forget to hold on to the beauty and good that's been planted in us as well, remembering all the positive ways we have been touched by strangers and loved ones alike. In "Kindness," Rosemerry Wahtola Trommer invites us to see how these kindnesses might rise up again in us later on like tulips—"a bit of beauty" that has blossomed from the root of "a kind word, perhaps, or a touch, the gift of their time or their smile." The smallest gifts can transform the ground that we are into something new, until some long-ago tenderness "emerges again, pushing aside the dead leaves, insisting on loveliness," perhaps when someone else needs it the most. The final lines of the poem remind us that when we can notice the fruits of some past kindness in ourselves, this becomes "a celebration of the one who planted it" as well as "the one who perceives it." We can rejoice in recognizing how we have "grown" like those tulips because of the caring attention of the many who came before us.

Invitation for Writing and Reflection

Consider all the ways that others have planted "a bit of beauty" in you, and all the many kindnesses you have offered others. How has your own life changed as a result of such simple, caring actions?

Kai Coggin

INTO WILDFLOWER INTO FIELD

it's dusk and I watch you
water our newly-planted garden,
the radish and arugula
are first to push up through the soil,
green hands in prayer
unfolding toward sun and sky
and I sit on the side and write
as you coax them
toward you

it's like you're singing
invisibly to the sleeping bed of seeds
like I can see the vibration of
your gentle harvest hope

my own fingers
begin searching the earth
my body bends toward the light
of you
I green into a personal spring
my seeds
break open again
and again
searching for sun and sky *(your eyes)*

constant gardener—
you water the drought of me

into wildflower
into royal meadow
into fields and fields and fields

did you ever think our lives
would bloom into this?

on the ridge-line
the setting day paints
us in an impermanent gold
but even now in the darkest dark of night
everything around us is aglow

Laura Budofsky Wisniewski

A BEGINNER'S GUIDE TO GARDENING ALONE

Because a hummingbird perched
on a high branch of the alder,
because I raised my eyes
from the ground of my obsessions
I saw her linger.
Because a green tinged feather causes this world
with its fools' winds, with its flawed light
with its thrusts, its false fledges,
a red hibiscus opened.
Its petals were like palms parting,
like the lips of the world parting.
Because a teardrop of nectar ran
from the deep mine of the flower
onto its trembling stamen,
onto its stigma, its muteness,
onto its speckled rubies,
I brought my hands together.
Between my palms, there formed
a dark cave of prayer. Between my lips,
there slipped a faint breath of flight.

Heather Lanier

THE HEARTBEAT OF MY UNBORN CHILD

used to be a flutter, a hummingbird's
blurry wing buzzing
a half-inch of spring,

is now a runner
barefoot through a wet forest.

Determined. Compelled
by what, I wonder?
Chasing nothing but another
and another and another beat?
The chance to be

in a new now?
The want, my barely baby, as simple as that
single grass blade being,
in this new season of green,
its thin bendable self in the sun?

Mary Elder Jacobsen

SPONGE BATH

At first, to let him know I'm here,
I start with song, a kind of coo,
or croon. My voice breaks,
morning waking into lullaby.
I test the water at my wrist,
here, the bare pulse point.
Not hot. Not cold. Just warm.
I dip the soft infant cloth into
the wash basin, swish, and squeeze.
Damp, not dripping. I bring
some order to our routine, begin
with crown, brow, temples.
Traveling the topography
of the face—ears, eyes,
mouth, nose—all our animal
pathways, I grow humbled
by the whole of us, this space
I find myself within, caring for
another being, my newborn
at home, only a few days old,
a kind of gift that overwhelms,
to know we've only just begun
to say hello.

Laura Grace Weldon

MOST IMPORTANT WORD

Before teaching my first child
all eight letters of his name,
I showed him how to write
the most important word.

Tongue tucked against upper lip,
pencil tight in soft four-year-old fingers,
he copied my letters. Drew
a chairback with wobbly seat,
tippy egg, empty ice cream cone,
pitchfork without a handle.

That spells *LOVE*, I told him.
He wrote it on crayoned pictures,
breath-fogged windows,
chalked sidewalks.
He wrote it alongside the next words
he learned—*love mom, love dad, love tree,
love* squeezed next to his own name.

Shapes unlocked into symbols,
soon he read aloud stories
to go with pictures he drew.
Now I teach his daughter
that first magical word.
She concentrates,
lines rollicking onto the paper,
tongue curled against her lip.

James Crews

ONLY LOVE

Only love is big enough to hold all the pain of this world.
—*Sharon Salzberg*

And so I imagine the entire earth
as one beating heart held in the space
of this universe, inside a larger body
we can't fathom, filling with enough
love to lead each of us out of the cave
of our personal pain and into the light—
enough love to lead all humans as one
out of collective fear, rage, and hate
into a place of peace that is found only
within our own hearts, beating in sync
with the pulse of this planet we were
born to inhabit, despite the daily storms
which overtake us and make us forget
we are the lifeblood pumped into these
veins, every particle of love we generate
running into rivers, lakes, and creeks,
evaporating into the air we breathe,
give back, and breathe again.

David Van Houten

BREATHE

beside a dry river wash
stands a grove of desert pines

steadfast trunks rise from roots
braided deep within the earth

branches stretch overhead
arc in full canopy

offer shelter from relentless heat
amid streams of filtered sunlight

ground dense with needlework
no footstep is heard

boughs beckon in the breeze
move me to pause

ease into their embrace
accept their generosity

surrender
to shaded sanctuary

January Gill O'Neil

ELATION

In the city's center is an unwalled forest:
a dense plot of cedars so thick their canopy
keeps light from reaching the ground.

We gaze at the stretched-out stalks—
Etiolation, you say, pointing skyward,
but all I hear is *elation*.

It's the elongation of stems,
the branches growing up, not out,
their long trunks turned white

from too little light. Tolerant trees.
They claim this space as their own,
making the most of what's given them.

Their back and forth sway moves us.
We listen to spindly trees creaking—
rocking chairs on a wooden porch,

the sound of a cello's drawn breath,
the clatter of branches like the chatter
between old, coupled voices

when no one is around.

MY DAUGHTER MEETS MY WHITE PINE

That was my woodlot; that was my lot in the woods. The
silvery needles of the pine straining the light.
—*Henry David Thoreau*

If we added together your age
and mine, this pine is older,
destined to outlive us both.
Touch its bark,
trace the puzzle pieces.
A thin maple twines beside
and up inside the pine:
maple's red-gold flaunting
its place within wind-blown silver.

You study the bowing-to-earth gnarled
branching of this wolf tree, an old one spared
to leave shade for grazers when the woods
was cleared for pasture, a century older
than other trees in the forest.

You see my sacred tree as a scientist does;
I see this as a mother.

We are not so different—
years from now, return,
to sit under one limb or the other
to remember me,
after the crickets stop singing.

Julie Cadwallader Staub

TURNING

There comes a time in every fall
before the leaves begin to turn
when blackbirds group and flock and gather
choosing a tree, a branch, together
to click and call and chorus and clamor
announcing the season has come for travel.

Then comes a time when all those birds
without a sound or backward glance
pour from every branch and limb
into the air, as if on a whim
but it's a dynamic, choreographed mass
a swoop, a swerve, a mystery, a dance

and now the tree stands breathless, amazed
at how it was chosen, how it was changed.

Ingrid Goff-Maidoff

PEACE CAME TODAY

Peace came today
through a slender breeze.
Stopping for a moment in the field,
I felt the clouds of my mind
gently lift and move along.
Some days it happens like this—
with simplicity, lightness, ease.

Others, I must haul my complaints
to the ocean's edge,
look out across the blue water,
out beyond I know not what,
somewhere past the horizon,
and beseech, and invoke, and beg,
and breathe the salt air in
until, quieted again, I am opened
with no words to pour in between
this life and the life I am living.

Nothing left to long for.
Nothing left to say.

Kim Stafford

A CHAIR BY THE CREEK

Someone spoke twisted words to hurt you,
control you, tarnish your name. Good thing
you have this chair out under the cottonwoods
where leaves swivel trouble away.

A nosey neighbor shouts across the property line—
something about your right to be. Good thing those
words were swallowed by the friendly rattle
and chuckle of the creek.

Settled in your chair, enchanted by moving water,
your thoughts turn green, your heart fills with
slanted sunlight, whisper of aspen. You put all
words of envy, anger, and greed into the sound

of moving water, and listen as they flow away.

Danny Dover

FLOODWOOD POND

Before a shattered world
can begin to heal
it might first float here
amid moss and minnows
in the shimmering mist
of an approaching dawn.

We have only this body
and only one earth
made from flesh and blood
of porous mountains
where a doubtful heart
may soak in warm
uncertainty.

You could stay awhile
with breath and gravity
your only guides
a primal sound
pooling and rising
from somewhere deep
within your belly.

And if you pray to stars
then here is the infinite
dance of light
upon a shrine
of rippling water.

Ted Kooser

FILLING THE CANDLES

The eight candles that stand at the altar
aren't candles at all, but oil lamps
in the waxy white raiment of candles.

A woman has come, through snow, alone
on Saturday, to fill them, a plastic jug
in one hand, a funnel and rag in the other.

From a high window, soft hands of light,
in reds, blues and greens, pat snow
from the sleeves of her winter parka,

brush flakes from her silvery hair
as she moves from wick to wick to wick,
lifting the brass caps, trickling the oil.

The church is otherwise empty, dark
and cold, but now those eight flames burn
within her as she caps and tilts the jug

into the light to see how much is gone,
the day, too, halfway gone, not spilled
but used, a little warmth within it.

Mary Ray Goehring

PINCH POT

It fits perfectly
into the cup of my hands
when they are pressed together as if holding
precious water gathered fresh
from a clear ice-capped mountain stream

A pinch pot
made by my son in high school
terra cotta colored clay
carefully smoothed by his hands
rounded on the bottom like a bowl
or an ancient Anasazi vessel

Inside
an indigo blue glazed line
spirals away from the center
as if this opening
this empty space
can be forever filled
to overflowing

Into the cradle of my hands
it conjoins
like a prayer
finally answered

Margaret Hasse

CLOTHING

Clothes press against
the glass window
of a washing machine
like faces in the rain.

After they've spun
in the big dryer, I fold
my baby's plush onesies,
my son's favorite jeans,
and t-shirts my husband
taught me to roll
like window shades
when it's my turn
to do the laundry.

I stack up the items
then hug everything
to my chest, smelling
warm clean cotton
that covers the ones I love.

Angela Narciso Torres

CHORE

My friend turns anything into
prayer. Sweeping the leaves, shaving
his beard, washing dishes—

every act a purging
of what doesn't serve. Today
I'm folding laundry. I start with jeans,

crisp from the dryer, smoothing the creases
then draping them on wooden hangers.
Shaking wrinkles from the sheets, I square

the corners the way Mother taught.
White T-shirts stacked flat on a shelf,
sundresses on felt hangers, sweaters

nestled in drawers. I find a place
for every blouse, every scarf, until
it feels inevitable. *Order our days—*

the remnant floats up from decades
of Sundays like words of a forgotten
song—*in Your peace*. My mantra:

fold, hang, repeat, the hamper
half-empty, the bureau warm
with balled-up socks.

REFLECTIVE PAUSE

The Sacred Everyday

By describing how a friend can turn any chore into a form of prayer, and then showing us how she does this simply by folding laundry, Angela Narciso Torres teaches us to transform ordinary tasks of our lives into acts of generosity. She writes so carefully and lovingly of how she smoothes, folds, stacks, and drapes all of her family's clothing, we can't help but feel a sense of calm and order emanating from this simple scene. The gateway to a mindful poem that stays with the reader is often strong sensory details; and the sense that stands out in this poem is that of touch and texture. Notice how those creased jeans, felt hangers, and "sweaters nestled in drawers" all come to physical life, until we reach the final, vivid lines describing the bureau now "warm with balled-up socks." That warmth passes not only to the dresser she's filling with folded clothing but also to the reader as we feel those socks fresh from the dryer, each one blessed for a moment by the heat of her attentive touch, turning what could have been an unpleasant chore into a kindness that she offers her family.

Invitation for Writing and Reflection

How might you bring a sense of the sacred and reverence to the repetitive tasks you have to complete each day? Is there some chore that has been transformed for you into an act of generosity or devotion, a kind of offering?

Twyla M. Hansen

TRYING TO PRAY

With my arms raised in a vee,
I gather the heavens and bring
my hands down slow together,
press palms and bow my head.

I try to forget the suffering,
the wars, the ravage of land
that threatens songbirds,
butterflies, and pollinators.

The ghosts of their wings flutter
past my closed eyes as I breathe
the spirit of seasons, the stirrings
in soil, trees moving with sap.

With my third eye, I conjure
the red fox, its healthy tail, recount
the good of this world, the farmer
tending her tomatoes, the beans

dazzled green *al dente* in butter,
salt and pepper, cows munching
on grass. The orb of sun-gold
from which all bounty flows.

Joy Harjo

FOR KEEPS

Sun makes the day new.
Tiny green plants emerge from earth.
Birds are singing the sky into place.
There is nowhere else I want to be but here.
I lean into the rhythm of your heart to see where it will
    take us.
We gallop into a warm, southern wind.
I link my legs to yours and we ride together,
Toward the ancient encampment of our relatives.
Where have you been? they ask.
And what has taken you so long?
That night after eating, singing, and dancing
We lay together under the stars.
We know ourselves to be part of mystery.
It is unspeakable.
It is everlasting.
It is for keeps.

Barbara Crooker

SUSTENANCE

The sky hangs up its starry pictures: a swan,
a crab, a horse. And even though you're
three hundred miles away, I know you see
them, too. Right now, my side
of the bed is empty, a clear blue lake
of flannel. The distance yawns and stretches.
It's hard to remember we swim in an ocean
of great love, so easy to fall into bickering
like little birds at the feeder fighting over proso
and millet, unaware of how large the bag of grain is,
a river of golden seeds, that the harvest was plentiful,
the corn is in the barn, and whenever we're hungry,
a dipperful of just what we need will be spilled . . .

Ruth Arnison

TWENTY YEARS OF LONGING

She leans back.
His arms curl around
holding her against him.

She releases twenty years
of longing to the wind and grabs from it
a new breath.

His face nuzzles into her hair,
fingertips surfing over the waves of connection.
She turns, molding her face into his.

Bare feet sinking into the wet sand,
tangled talkative toes expressing love
as they breathe into each other's bloodstream.

Curtained by windblown hair
their mouths merge, eyes blinded as tongues braille
each other's senses, finding their way home.

Danusha Laméris

THE HEART IS NOT

A pocket. A thing that
can be turned inside out
by anybody's hand. Not
a place for pebbles or loose
change. Not to carry old
receipts. It does not tear
at the seam. It doesn't have
a seam. It cannot be torn.

Laura Foley

LEARNING BY HEART

I was seven, couldn't sleep,
fearing my French teacher,
afraid I couldn't learn
a line I had to memorize.

Mom, trilling the night's
loneliest hour, at the piano,
made up a lilting song,
to help me remember—

I did, and still do,
her voice etched in tenderness,
fingers running over the keys,
somewhere deep inside me.

BILLOWING OVERHEAD

Her absence is like the sky, spread over everything.
—*C.S. Lewis*

It's not your absence I feel,
but your presence, palpable,
still snoring on the sofa
after chemo.

You are not missing
from any moment I breathe.

You exist.

In the painting you bought on a trip to Spain.
The chipped blue mug from your alma mater.
Broadway tickets I found in a drawer.

You are with me.

On the grocery shelf
beside those square orange crackers
you ate by the box.

In the sky,
billowing overhead,
declaring your existence
as someone still loved
on this earth.

Penny Harter

TWO METEORS

Two meteors flared last night, flamed above
the twilit trees, their arcing signatures dropping
so quickly they sputtered out and died.

Driving on, I thought that we must burn through
whatever sorrows ride our shoulders, or learn to
carry them like that young turtle I saw today

crossing the road before me, bearing his shell.
I did not stop to help, only swerved to avoid him,
then looked in the rear-view mirror, hoping that

he was still on his way. And I wrapped a prayer
around his fragile back, blessing his stumpy legs
and plodding faith on that slowly darkening road.

Tom Hennen

MADE VISIBLE

The world is full of bodies. It's a happy thing and they should all be loved. Human bodies, raccoon bodies, blueberry and limestone bodies are the shapes we take when we want to be seen. How curious we are when we wake up and find ourselves in one of these new homes. The feel of snow, which we faintly remember, also the smell of wind, the sunshine's sweet taste. Sometimes I forget which body I'm in, like now, as I rest on my favorite log, an old aspen near Muddy Creek. The log, warm in the spring day, seems to lose more weight each year. It is dissolving as it dries. Before long it will be light enough to lift off the ground, rise past the treetops and into the sky, leaving behind the reminder that we are meant to spend our whole lives trembling in anticipation of the next instant.

Cornelius Eady

A SMALL MOMENT

I walk into the bakery next door
To my apartment. They are about
To pull some sort of toast with cheese
From the oven. When I ask:
What's that smell? I am being
A poet, I am asking

What everyone else in the shop
Wanted to ask, but somehow couldn't;
I am speaking on behalf of two other
Customers who wanted to buy the
Name of it. I ask the woman
Behind the counter for a percentage
Of her sale. Am I flirting?
Am I happy because the days
Are longer? Here's what

She does: She takes her time
Choosing the slices. "I am picking
Out the good ones," she tells me. It's
April 14th. Spring, with five to ten
Degrees to go. Some days, I feel my duty;
Some days, I love my work.

Zoe Higgins

ODE

Here's to everything undone today:
laundry left damp in the machine,
the relatives unrung, the kitchen
drawer not sorted; here's to jeans
unpatched and buttons missing,
the dirty dishes, the novel
not yet started. To Christmas
cards unsent in March, to emails
marked unread. To friends unmet
and deadlines unaddressed;
to every item not crossed off the list;
to everything still left, ignored, put off:
it is enough.

Donna Hilbert

CREDO

I believe in the Tuesdays
and Wednesdays of life,
the tuna sandwich lunches
and TV after dinner.
I believe in coffee with hot milk
and peanut butter toast,
Rosé wine in summer
and Burgundy in winter.
I am not in love with holidays,
birthdays—nothing special—
and weekends are just days
numbered six and seven,
though my love
dozing over TV golf
while I work the Sunday puzzle
might be all I need of life
and all I ask of heaven.

James Crews

SELF-CARE

Some days it feels like a foreign language
I'm asked to practice, with new words
for happiness, work, and love. I'm still learning
how to say: a cup of tea for no reason,
what to call the extra honey I drizzle in,
how to label the relentless urge to do more
and more as *useless*. And how to translate
the heart's pounding message when it comes:
enough, enough. This morning, I search for words
to capture the glimmering sun as it lifts
above the mountains, clouds already closing in
as fat droplets of rain darken the deck.
I'm learning to call this stillness self-care too,
just standing here, as goldfinches scatter up
from around the feeder like broken pieces
of bright yellow stained-glass, reassembling
in the sheltering arms of a maple.

Reassembling the Parts

In my poem "Self-Care," I am thinking about the habits of busyness and how self-care is a new language I have to learn again and again. Often, after a stressful time, I need space and stillness to let go of the frenetic energy coursing through my body. This takes hours of gentle living and what can feel like indulgence to the logical mind, even when the heart tells me I've had enough. But if I sit on the back porch with a cup of tea, just watching chipmunks and squirrels scurry through the yard—if I hit the pause button—I always return to life and work refreshed, less driven by pressure and fear. If I take a moment to appreciate the sunrise, a new one every day, or stop at the kitchen window to note the comings and goings of birds at the feeder, I punctuate my endless stream of thinking with a little space outside of time. During these slower moments of what I call "soul time," gratitude often slips in. My problems don't disappear, but are right-sized in the container of a mind that takes in the vastness of the world around me. The parts that feel shattered and scattered slowly reassemble, clicking back into place like the pieces of a jigsaw puzzle that reveals a fuller picture of life.

Invitation for Writing and Reflection
Can you recall an instance when you were especially kind to yourself, perhaps taking the time and making space for more gratitude in your days?

January Gill O'Neil

SUNDAY

You are the start of the week
or the end of it, and according
to The Beatles you creep in
like a nun. You're the second
full day the kids have been
away with their father, the second
full day of an empty house.
Sunday, I've missed you. I've been
sitting in the backyard with a glass
of Pinot waiting for your arrival.
Did you know the first Sweet 100s
are turning red in the garden,
but the lettuce has grown
too bitter to eat. I am looking
up at the bluest sky I have ever seen,
cerulean blue, a heaven sky
no one would believe I was under.
You are my witness. No day
is promised. You are absolution.
You are my unwritten to-do list,
my dishes in the sink, my brownie
breakfast, my braless day.

Laura Grace Weldon

THURSDAY MORNING

Darkness frees me to stand nightgowned
on the porch, watch
the dogs merge into shadow,
snuffle, pee, reappear.

I stretch, inhale summer's warm weight,
imagine staying in this spot
while what has to be done
swirls by undone.

I imagine a taproot growing down my spine,
out my feet, through the porch floor
and deep underground,
rootlets reaching all directions.

Imagine remaining here so long
I fade from sight, although
everyone crossing this portal
pauses as they pass through my arms.

Joy Gaines-Friedler

TOUCH

A chickadee lands in your hand
its body a buoy.

It grips your finger. You
don't hold it. It holds you.

It is a kiss, both hard & soft,
both lip & bone.

On your way about your life,
at the mailbox or a stop light,

your body remembers
those feathers. That touch & others.

Heather Swan

ON LIGHTNESS

Outside my window,
a wren alights
on a fiddlehead fern,
and the plant is forced
to bend its green spine.
As he rests there,
the air never leaves
the bird's body—
the way he floats
through trees. And then
he takes to the sky again,
and the fern sways
upright, opening its arms,
once again, to the sun.
If only it could always
be like this:
the burden of one
never breaking another.

José A. Alcantara

DIVORCE

He has flown headfirst against the glass
and now lies stunned on the stone patio,
nothing moving but his quick beating heart.
So you go to him, pick up his delicate
body and hold him in the cupped palms
of your hands. You have always known
he was beautiful, but it's only now, in his stillness,
in his vulnerability, that you see the miracle
of his being, how so much life fits in so small
a space. And so you wait, keeping him warm
against the unseasonable cold, trusting that
when the time is right, when he has recovered
both his strength and his sense of up and down,
he will gather himself, flutter once or twice,
and then rise, a streak of dazzling
color against a slowly lifting sky.

Susan Moorhead

SHIFT

If you hold a sparrow
in the cup of your hand,
a found one, stunned
by the smash of glass
that was window not sky,
forever after
when you see a sparrow,
you'll remember
the feel of the feather-soft body,
the tiny heart beating against
your fingers.

Tracy K. Smith

SONG

I think of your hands all those years ago
Learning to maneuver a pencil, or struggling
To fasten a coat. The hands you'd sit on in class,
The nails you chewed absently. The clumsy authority
With which they'd sail to the air when they knew
You knew the answer. I think of them lying empty
At night, of the fingers wrangling something
From your nose, or buried in the cave of your ear.
All the things they did cautiously, pointedly,
Obedient to the suddenest whim. Their shames.
How they failed. What they won't forget year after year.
Or now. Resting on the wheel or the edge of your knee.
I am trying to decide what they feel when they wake up
And discover my body is near. Before touch.
Pushing off the ledge of the easy quiet dancing between us.

Mark Nepo

DRINKING THERE

No matter how many conversations I
start, they all end with me kneeling at
the same deep well. And drinking there,
I remember who I am. I rise from that
drinking able to see, again, that we are
at heart the same. And the secret wound
you show me there is my wound which I
have hidden for so long. And the secret
joy you bring into the open is my joy
which I thought I had lost. Experience
has us meet in the most unexpected ways.
Until we're forced to show the soft center
that never dies. Until our soul appears in
the world like a pearl before it hardens.
Until the gift of life stirs in our hand
like a tuft of feathers that needs to
be loved into a wing.

Susan Musgrave

MORE THAN SEEING

There is a moment before the kingfisher dives,
the eagle swoops, the small green ducks disappear
like the breeze in the low hanging cedar branches
over the river; there is a moment before I name
the kingfisher, the eagle, the ducks when I am not
the observer, I am the dart of light, rush of wings,
the trusting wind; I am grace: an end of living
in awe of things, a beginning of living with them.

Julia Fehrenbacher

THE MOST IMPORTANT THING

I am making a home inside myself. A shelter
of kindness where everything
is forgiven, everything allowed—a quiet patch
of sunlight to stretch out without hurry,
where all that has been banished and buried
is welcomed, spoken, listened to—released.

A fiercely friendly place I can claim as my very own.

I am throwing arms open
to the whole of myself—especially the fearful,
fault-finding, falling apart, unfinished parts, knowing
every seed and weed, every drop
of rain, has made the soil richer.

I will light a candle, pour a hot cup of tea, gather
around the warmth of my own blazing fire. I will howl
if I want to, knowing this flame can burn through
any perceived problem, any prescribed perfectionism,
any lying limitation, every heavy thing.

I am making a home inside myself
where grace blooms in grand and glorious
abundance, a shelter of kindness that grows
all the truest things.

I whisper hallelujah to the friendly
sky. Watch now as I burst into blossom.

Julia Alvarez

VAIN DOUBTS

Years ago now—a breezy, bygone day,
walking a city street, my hair tossing,
feeling the beauty of my young body,
that animal friskiness triggered by spring,
I glanced admiringly at my reflection
in a storefront window, tossing my head
to watch that mirrored waving of a mane
I thought my best feature—when a young man
coming in my direction barred my way.
Glaring at me, he uttered, "Vanity!"

And I was stopped in my mindless moment
of physical joy, shamed to associate
that deadly sin with the upsurge of life
and self-love I'd been feeling, never doubting
my urban prophet had been right. Vanity—
so this was what that ugly sin felt like!
In his disgust, I heard the click of keys
in convents, harems, attics, marriages,
down the generations, doors closing on
bodies that could give both pleasure and life.

Now that the years have granted me release
from such vain doubts, I'd like to post myself
at slumber parties, bathrooms, dressing rooms,
wherever young girls gather, frowning at
their wrong-size figures, blah hair, blemished skin—
already taught to find fault or disguise
joy in their bodies. I'd like to be the voice
that drowns out their self-doubt, singing in praise
of what I couldn't see when I was young:
we're simply beautiful, just as we are.

Molly Fisk

BEFORE I GAINED ALL THIS WEIGHT

I was so self-conscious I could barely
walk into town for fear people
would stare. I thought I was hideous,
unlovable. Now I want to shake
that poor girl, even though it wasn't
her fault, so afraid to be human—
rattle her cage of good grades, self-
tanning lotion and green eye-liner,
fast-acting depilatory cream, tell her
to smile for God's sake and kiss
the next boy she sees, life is shorter
than anyone imagines. Silver planes
plummet from clean skies, cancer gnaws
the marrow of even younger bones
than yours, wake up! There's still time!
Everything around you is unbelievably
beautiful.

Ross Gay

THANK YOU

If you find yourself half naked
and barefoot in the frosty grass, hearing,
again, the earth's great, sonorous moan that says
you are the air of the now and gone, that says
all you love will turn to dust,
and will meet you there, do not
raise your fist. Do not raise
your small voice against it. And do not
take cover. Instead, curl your toes
into the grass, watch the cloud
ascending from your lips. Walk
through the garden's dormant splendor.
Say only, thank you.
Thank you.

Lorna Crozier

SMALL LESSON

Hoarfrost
feathering the window
and behind that

a high cloud
and behind that
the winter moon.

Three things without
their own light
yet how they shine.

Leah Naomi Green

THE AGE OF AFFECTION

Thank you, moon, for following
across the pond

while I walked,
for bringing me

to the shore
to say goodnight.

The affection
of your speech

is inside me.
That is exactly where I want it.

Has anyone I've loved
ever been

anywhere else?
You followed over the field too,

and into the house,
though the grass

did not reflect you,
or the milky way rising,

as I can sometimes witness
even from inside it.

Barbara Crooker

FORSYTHIA

What must it feel like
after months of existing
as bare brown sticks,
all reasonable hope
of blossoming lost,
to suddenly, one warm
April morning, burst
into wild yellow song,
hundreds of tiny prayer
flags rippling in the still-
cold wind, the only flash
of color in the dull yard,
these small scraps of light,
something we might
hold on to.

Karen Craigo

LAST SCRAPS OF COLOR IN MISSOURI

Today I passed a stand
of trees: tall, closely packed,
bare and almost black
from rain. But underneath,
I saw smaller trees, just
getting started on their slow
snatch-and-grab of sky,
and I saw these were golden
still, and they glowed
like campfires in the dark.
Lately I'd been wanting
a little light — and there it was,
and all I had to do was turn
my gaze a few degrees
from center. Some blessings
find us when we move to them —
they're waiting only to be seen.
Near the end of a difficult year,
may we spot the light,
as we breathe in prayer
or supplication: *Show me,
show me, show me.*

Ted Kooser

IT DOESN'T TAKE MUCH

Maybe an hour before sunrise, driving alone
on the way to reach somewhere, seeing,
set back from the highway, the dark shape
of a farmhouse up against deeper darkness,
a light in one window. Or farther along

into a gray, watery dawn, passing
a McDonald's, lighted bright as a city,
and seeing one man, in ball cap, alone
in a booth, not looking down at his table
but ahead, over the empty booths. Or

maybe an hour farther, in full daylight,
at a place where a bus stops, seeing
a woman somewhere in her forties,
dressed for cold, wearing white ear muffs,
a red and white team jacket, blue jeans

and Muk Luks, one knit mitten holding
a slack empty mitten, her bare hand
extended, pinching a lit cigarette,
dry leaves—the whole deck of a new day—
fanned out face-down in the gutter, but

she's not stooping to turn over a card,
but instead watching a long ash grow
even longer at the ends of her fingers.
Just that much might be enough for one
morning to make you feel part of it all.

REFLECTIVE PAUSE

Part of It All Again

In "It Doesn't Take Much," Ted Kooser shows us how simply noticing the people we encounter, and seeing them in all their uniqueness and humanity, can become a form of kindness. The speaker of this poem at first seems lonely as he drives aimlessly "into a gray, watery dawn," yet even the "bright city" of a fast-food restaurant, and the man at a booth inside, can remind him he's not entirely alone in the world. When we're feeling disconnected, we often forget that one of the surest ways to lift ourselves out of despair is to give our attention to the people around us. Instead of just speeding past the woman he sees waiting at a bus stop, for instance, he takes in all of her details, from how she's dressed to the way she's "pinching a lit cigarette." Though he has not spoken to the man and woman he describes, by the end of the poem, he nevertheless feels more connected to the larger world, "part of it all" again, having shifted his focus away from himself and his own troubles to what's around him, remembering that there are countless stories contained in each person we meet, even if we do only briefly glimpse them as we move through our lives.

Invitation for Writing and Reflection

The next time you find yourself struggling or distracted, absorbed in your own thoughts and worries, take a notebook or laptop out into the world, and truly notice the people who cross your path. Who stands out to you, and what details might give you a glimpse into their story?

Ellen Bass

THE THING IS

to love life, to love it even
when you have no stomach for it
and everything you've held dear
crumbles like burnt paper in your hands,
your throat filled with the silt of it.
When grief sits with you, its tropical heat
thickening the air, heavy as water
more fit for gills than lungs;
when grief weights you down like your own flesh
only more of it, an obesity of grief,
you think, *How can a body withstand this?*
Then you hold life like a face
between your palms, a plain face,
no charming smile, no violet eyes,
and you say, yes, I will take you
I will love you, again.

James Crews

SELF-COMPASSION

My friend and I snickered the first time
we heard the meditation teacher, a grown man,
call himself *honey*, with a hand placed
over his heart to illustrate how we too
might become more gentle with ourselves
and our runaway minds. It's been years
since we sat with legs twisted on cushions,
holding back our laughter, but today
I found myself crouched on the floor again,
not meditating exactly, just agreeing
to be still, saying *honey* to myself each time
I thought about my husband splayed
on the couch with aching joints and fever
from a tick bite—what if he never gets better?—
or considered the threat of more wildfires,
the possible collapse of the Gulf Stream,
then remembered that in a few more minutes,
I'd have to climb down to the cellar and empty
the bucket I placed beneath a leaky pipe
that can't be fixed until next week. How long
does any of us really have before the body
begins to break down and empty its mysteries
into the air? Oh *honey*, I said—for once

without a trace of irony or blush of shame—
the touch of my own hand on my chest
like that of a stranger, oddly comforting
in spite of the facts.

Kelli Russell Agodon

PRAISE

Find me wild about stir-fry, about red velvet
sofas and the people who sleep inside books
and dream about commas. We are flooded
with forgetfulness, with fallen plum blossoms
misspelling our names on the driveway. Praise
our too many expectations, how we overestimate
the weather, each other, overestimate how deer
will appear if we arrive with food. Because reality
can be a knife, we sometimes ache to tear open
the tea bag, the ketchup packet, because wine
arrives ready to be poured, we are foolish
and happy—though our clothes do not fit,
we return to being alive and living
between roadblocks and detours, driving
our fingers into the edge of each other's
pockets. Praise the bare trees that tried
to spell our names for their belief
they could—spells and misspellings,
fail and fail better, how lucky we are
just to be here, both of us touching each other
through these words, with all this exasperating joy.

Dorianne Laux

JOY

Even when the gods have driven you
from your home, your friends, the tree
you planted brought down by storm,
drought, chain saw, beetles, even

when you've been scrubbed
hollow by confusion, loss,
accept joy, those unbidden
moments of surcease—

the quiet unfolding
around your shoulders
like a shawl, the warmth
that doesn't turn to burning.

When the itch has stopped, the cough,
the throb, the heart's steady beat
resumed, the barn door

open to the shade, the horse inside
waiting for your touch, apple
in your pocket pocked, riddled

the last to fall, the season
done. As you would accept
air into your lungs, without
thinking, not counting

each breath. As you accepted
the earth the first time you stood
up on it and it held you, how it was

just there, a solid miracle,
gravity something you would
learn about only later
and still be amazed.

Jack Ridl

TAKE LOVE FOR GRANTED

Assume it's in the kitchen,
under the couch, high
in the pine tree out back,
behind the paint cans
in the garage. Don't try
proving your love
is bigger than the Grand
Canyon, the Milky Way,
the urban sprawl of L.A.
Take it for granted. Take it
out with the garbage. Bring
it in with the takeout. Take
it for a walk with the dog.
Wake it every day, say,
"Good morning." Then
make the coffee. Warm
the cups. Don't expect much
of the day. Be glad when
you make it back to bed.
Be glad he threw out that
box of old hats. Be glad
she leaves her shoes
in the hall. Snow will
come. Spring will show up.
Summer will be humid.
The leaves will fall

in the fall. That's more
than you need. We can
love anybody, even
everybody. But *you*
can love the silence,
sighing and saying to
yourself, "That' s her."
"That's him." Then to
each other, "I know!
Let's go out for breakfast!"

Terri Kirby Erickson

FREE BREAKFAST

The Springhill Suites free breakfast area
was filling up fast when a man carrying his
disabled young son lowered him into his
chair, the same way an expert pilot's airplane
kisses the runway when it lands. And all the
while, the man whispered into his boy's ear,
perhaps telling him about the waffle maker
that was such a hit with the children gathered
around it, or sharing the family's plans for the
day as they traveled to wherever they were
going. Whatever was said, the boy's face was
alight with some anticipated happiness. And
the father, soon joined by the mother, seemed
intent on providing it. So beautiful they all
were, it was hard to concentrate on our eggs
and buttered toast, to look away when his
parents placed their hands on the little boy's
shoulders and smiled at one another, as if
they were the luckiest people in the room.

Annie Lighthart

PASSENGER

This child between us here in our dark bed asks nothing
but to be held all night, to burrow, to stay wedged
and warmed by our bodies until day.
Tomorrow he will demand more jam, will need
new shoes, will drop the toast and plate to the floor.
But just now, here, breathing softly between us,
he is a small Venetian gondolier refusing pay,
taking us back and forth all night singing
underneath the Bridge of Sighs.

Christine Stewart-Nuñez

SITE PLANNING

As I cross this network of interstates
driving toward home, I'm dried out
of words until I hear *neural network*
on the radio, and I picture a lake
with streams that branch and taper.
Net. Work. My mother-made nets
for my oldest son: family, stories,
photos, arms reaching, reaching.
Across chasms, I've woven lifelines
to schools, doctors, and specialists
so he won't fall through. And as I drive
past fields so flooded I can't see
where they thin or end, I recall
the pervasiveness of his seizures—
one per minute when he slept.
They're receding now, but what
will they leave when they've dried up?
Some say new knowledge and new
memories; I imagine sunflower fields.
What work will my nets do then?
Perhaps he'll make his own trawls
weave into mine. Either way, each day
brings a facet of him to the surface,
polished and gleaming.

Laura Foley

A PERFECT ARC

I remember the first time he dove.
He was five and we were at a swimming pool
and I said: you tip your head down as you are going in,
while your feet go up.

And then his lithe little body did it exactly right,
a perfect dive, sliding downward, arcing without a wave,
and I just stood
amazed and without words
as his blond head came up again
and today

I watched him for the longest time as he walked
firm and upright along the street,
with backpack, guitar, all he needs,
blossoming outward in a perfect arc,
a graceful turning
away from me.

Michael Simms

THE SUMMER YOU LEARNED TO SWIM

for Lea

The summer you learned to swim
was the summer I learned to be at peace with myself.
In May you were afraid to put your face in the water
but by August, I was standing in the pool once more
when you dove in, then retreated to the wall saying,
You forgot to say Sugar! So I said Come on Sugar, you can
    do it,
and you pushed off and swam to me and held on
laughing, your hair stuck to your cheeks—
you hiccuped with joy and swam off again.
And I dove in too, trying new things.
I tried not giving advice. I tried waking early to pray. I tried
not rising in anger. Watching you I grew stronger—
your courage washed away my fear.
All day I worked hard thinking of you.
In the evening I walked the long hill home.
You were at the top, waving your small arms,
pittering down the slope to me and I lifted you high,
so high to the moon. That summer all the world
was soul and water, light glancing off peaks.
You learned the turtle, the cannonball, the froggy, and the
    flutter
and I learned to stand and wait for you to swim to me.

James Crews

THE POOL

Because he couldn't afford
the kidney-shaped, in-ground pool
we all wanted, my father went out
and bought a used galvanized pool
whose rusted rim I refused to touch.

As usual, he had a solution:
he split a length of black rubber hose
down the middle with his pocketknife
then stretched it over the rough sides,
inch by inch, until no rust showed.

Back then, I never thought such gestures
were selfless, evidence of what we call
unconditional love. But now I feel
my small hands gripping soft rubber,
and I see my father on the back porch,

cigarette hanging from his smiling lips
as he watches me lift myself
out of the pool, flinging cold water
from my goose-pimpled skin
as if I'd been reborn again.

Joyce Sutphen

CARRYING WATER TO THE FIELD

And on those hot afternoons in July,
when my father was out on the tractor
cultivating rows of corn, my mother
would send us out with a Mason jar
filled with ice and water, a dish towel
wrapped around it for insulation.

Like a rocket launched to an orbiting
planet, we would cut across the fields
in a trajectory calculated to intercept—
or, perhaps, even—surprise him
in his absorption with the row and the
turning always over earth beneath the blade.

He would look up and see us, throttle
down, stop, and step from the tractor
with the grace of a cowboy dismounting
his horse, and receive gratefully the jar
of water, ice cubes now melted into tiny
shards, drinking it down in a single gulp,
while we watched, mission accomplished.

David Romtvedt

AT THE CREEK

I go to the creek with my daughter.
We squat at the water's edge
and look around. Some pebbles,
a few sticks, a cottonwood leaf.
With these we make a tiny world
in which nothing moves.

Would that be heaven then
where all things come to rest?

It's as if I stand
once again by my desk
on the first day of school
and the teacher calls my name,
and I say, "Here."

She looks up and smiles
at me and I at her. "Here,"
I say again, "Here."

REFLECTIVE PAUSE

Would That Be Heaven?

David Romtvedt's poem begins with a father and daughter as they "squat at the water's edge," doing nothing but looking around at the seemingly plainer things of nature: "Some pebbles, a few sticks, a cottonwood leaf." And yet with these, they manage to create "a tiny world" of their own, separate from the often crowded, noisy environment many of us inhabit daily, our minds and bodies moving at speeds that leave us drained and disconnected. The speaker goes on to ask the question "Would that be heaven then where all things come to rest?" Yet he seems to know the answer, that this instant of shared time with his daughter is indeed a heaven that can never be re-created. The poem's gentle, careful touch, like that of a father leading his daughter by the hand through the woods, offers an unexpected but welcome peace to readers. The poet's question also reminds me of what St. Catherine of Siena once said: "All the way to heaven is heaven." So often, we think of paradise as some place other than where we are, even though the most lasting versions of heaven on Earth tend to be found in our own backyards, in our ordinary lives, when we pause long enough to say "Here" and "Here," over and over, calling our attention back to the now.

Invitation for Writing and Reflection

Think about a time when you discovered your own heaven embedded in a moment of togetherness with someone you cared about. What simple elements allowed you to build "a tiny world" of your own, even for just a few minutes?

Michael Kleber-Diggs

CONIFEROUS FATHERS

Let's fashion gentle fathers, expressive—holding us
how we wanted to be held before we could ask.

Singing off-key lullabies, written for us—songs
every evening, like possibilities. Fathers who say,

this is how you hold a baby, but never mention
a football. Say nothing in that moment, just bring

us to their chests naturally, without shyness.
Let's grow fathers from pine, not oak, coniferous

fathers raising us in their shade, fathers soft enough
to bend—fathers who love us like their fathers

couldn't. Fathers who can talk about menstruation
while playing a game of pepper in the front yard.

No, take baseball out. Let's discover a new sort—
fathers as varied and vast as the Superior Forest.

Let's kill off sternness and play down wisdom;
give us fathers of laughter and fathers who cry,

fathers who say *Check this out*, or *I'm scared*, or *I'm sorry*,
or *I don't know*. Give us fathers strong enough

to admit they want to be near us; they've always
wanted to be near us. Give us fathers desperate

for something different, not Johnny Appleseed,
not even Atticus Finch. No more rolling stones.

No more La-Z-Boy dads reading newspapers in
some other room. Let's create folklore side-by-side

in a garden singing psalms about abiding—just that,
abiding: being steadfast, present, evergreen, and

ethereal—let's make the old needles soft enough
for us to rest on, dream on, next to them.

Zeina Azzam

MY FATHER'S HANDS

They were not large, but thick
fleshy workers in the garden
nursing eggplants and fennel,
okra and chard,
digging and tilling and weeding,
making the soil an obliging host.

Maybe that's what made
his fingers rough in spots,
or maybe it was the constant leafing
through books: a loving lick
and a flip-flap of the page
in search of nuggets
that would be turned over and over
in his mind.

After he died
I found bookmarks between pages
carefully pointing
like tags next to seedlings in the earth:
These are the plants I hoped for.
These are the ideas that made me grow.

Li-Young Lee

EARLY IN THE MORNING

While the long grain is softening
in the water, gurgling
over a low stove flame, before
the salted Winter Vegetable is sliced
for breakfast, before the birds,
my mother glides an ivory comb
through her hair, heavy
and black as calligrapher's ink.

She sits at the foot of the bed.
My father watches, listens for
the music of comb
against hair.

My mother combs,
pulls her hair back
tight, rolls it
around two fingers, pins it
in a bun to the back of her head.
For half a hundred years she has done this.
My father likes to see it like this.
He says it is kempt.

But I know
it is because of the way

my mother's hair falls
when he pulls the pins out.
Easily, like the curtains
when they untie them in the evening.

Terri Kirby Erickson

NIGHT TALKS

When one would wake in the night, the other
followed. Then, in their bed, next to their window
that was always open, my mother and father
would talk to the sound of cars going by,
the hum of streetlights, the occasional bark
of a neighbor's dog. They spoke of high school
dances, family vacations, raising children,
being grandparents. And their faces, soft
with age and sleep, were hidden in the dark,
so they could speak at last of their lost son,
without any need to shield each other from
that pain. It must have been a relief to unpack
the shared sadness they courageously carried,
to put it down, if only for an hour. It was like
I could hear them from my own bed
across town, as I slipped into a deeper sleep,
reassured and comforted by their beloved
familiar voices echoing among the stars.

Julia Alvarez

LOVE PORTIONS

We're always fighting about household chores
but with this twist: we fight to do the work:
both wanting to fix dinner, mow the lawn,
haul the recycling boxes to the truck,
or wash the dishes when our guests depart.
I don't mean little spats, I mean real fights,
banged doors and harsh words over the soapsuds.
You did it last night! No fair, you shopped!
The feast spoils while we argue portions—
both so afraid of taking advantage.

But love should be unbalanced, a circus clown
carrying a tower of cups and saucers
who slips on a banana peel and lands
with every cup still full of hot coffee—
well, almost every cup. A field of seeds
pushing their green hopes through the frozen earth
to what might be spring or a springlike day
midwinter. Love ignores neat measures,
the waves leave ragged wet marks on the shore,
autumn lights one more fire in the maples.

Tonight, you say you're making our dinner
and won't let me so much as stir the sauce.
I march up to my study in a huff.
The oven buzzer sounds, the smells waft up
of something good I try hard to ignore

while I cook up my paper concoction.
Finally, you call me down to your chef d'oeuvre:
a three-course meal! I hand you mine, this poem.
Briefly, the scales balance between us:
food for the body, nurture for the soul.

Kate Duignan

GRANDMOTHER

When I was five
you taught me how to separate an egg.

I watched you tap it on the rim
of the bowl,
press your thumbs to the spot
and crack it clean in two.

You let me take the speckled shell
in my own hands
and rock the yolk back and forth,
quivering
as it slid from one half to the other,
a tiny yellow sun.

We put the splintered pieces
in the brown bin
for the compost

and the empty carton
in the red bin
for the incinerator.

In the garden,
the light went out of the golden elm.
We stood at the window.
The moon was a white cup.

The birds had gone to their nests, you said
and tomorrow would be a good day.

I spread my fingers on the dark glass.
Our cake, you said, would rise.

Todd Davis

HELIOTROPIC

In the evening light the dove's undersides
look yellow, and the bush that grows along
the porch has flowers red as a tanager's back.

At dinner, hummingbirds come to press needle-
beaks into trumpet-blossoms, the music
of their work drowning our conversation.

Why would anyone forsake this gospel of beauty?
Consider the bees covering the heads of sunflowers,
the sunflowers turning to follow the light.

When the world is pink, and the sun has begun
to sink to the other side of the earth, we walk
into fields tall with goldenrod to pick the daisies

my grandmother called moon-pennies, until the dark
makes it hard to see, and we must search for the light
glowing in the windows of the house to guide us home.

Marjorie Saiser

EVERYBODY IN THE SAME HOUSE

It was after someone's graduation
and even though some did
not want their picture taken,
I engineered the photo,
set up the tripod,
cajoled, insisted, got it:
faces in a jagged line,
the dog a blur,
and some of my love shining
(like now?) old-fashioned in my face.
That night everybody sleeping
under the same roof
in various cots and cubbyholes,
makeshift,
camping out.
This could be the occasion
we'll calculate from:
Remember that time
when we were all together?
That hour perhaps adjacent
to what the sacred might be:
a cave we have found, a temporary
stay, and the children
in their niches, full of sleep,
full of daring, full of risk,
turning over to other poses,
one by one, in safety.

Lahab Assef Al-Jundi

HOT TEA

Many years ago
my grandmother showed me
how to stir the sugar in my glass of hot tea.
She held the small spoon in her fingers
as if it were a feather,
lowered it until it rested on the bottom
then gently moved it from side to side.
Sugar swirled like a hazy cloud in amber sky,
then slowly faded away.
I had been spinning the spoon round and round
turning the hot liquid into a whirl,
spilling some of it over the rim.
Why is it every time I scoop a spoonful of sugar
to put in my tea
I go back to that sunny morning in Salamiyeh
sitting on colorful rugs under the big pine trees
in my grandparents' backyard?
I start to move the spoon in circles
then change,
side to side,
and momentarily get lost
in the turbulent sweet cloud
inside . . .

Gregory Orr

MORNING SONG

Sun on his face wakes him.
The boy makes his way down
through the spidery dark
of stairs to his breakfast
of cereal in a blue bowl.
He carries to the barn
a pie plate heaped
with vegetable scraps
for the three-legged deer.
As a fawn it stood still
and alone in high hay
while the red tractor
spiraled steadily inward,
mowing its precise swaths.
"I lived" is the song
the boy hears as the deer
hobbles toward him.
In the barn's huge gloom
light falls through the cracks
the way sword blades
pierce a magician's box.

HOW TO WAKE

Wake your brother with a soft voice by his pillow.
He has been very afraid.
Wake your mother with a kiss before calling her
    name.
Wake your grandfather with a touch on his knee,
    then wait—
he has far to come from the places he's been.
Wake the young dog with an open door, wake the
    old dog
with an outstretched hand. And yourself?
How will you wake that stubborn sleeper to life?
Look for a line let down through the water.
The silver hook is baited with a word.
Bite and awaken to that wild, clear sound.

Alice Wolf Gilborn

WAKE UP

On the radio this morning
they played something truly
remarkable—the sound of unknown

birds around the world awakening
to first light, starting in the east at dawn,
going west—hoots, howls, warbles,

then riffs and trills as another
contingent, another continent woke
up, until I could feel earth itself

turning with its brocade and bristle
of trees and music, that strange
and lovely communion of birds.

I wished and failed to name them.
Miffed, I let other thoughts jump in—
What were they doing? Why were they

singing? For mates, for space, for joy?
I heard only myself, my mind a darting
squirrel making a din, while the dawning

music slowly died. Maybe it's time to listen.
To think sunrise, birds, trees, earthturn.
To sing a little song at daybreak.

Alberto Ríos

DAWN CALLERS

The dawn callers and morning bringers,
I hear them as they intend themselves to be heard,

Quick sonic sparks in the morning dark,
Hard at the first work of building the great fire.

The soloist rooster in the distance,
The cheeping wrens, the stirring, gargling pigeons

Getting ready for the work of a difficult lifetime,
The first screet of the peahen in the far field,

All of it a great tag-of-sounds game engaging even the
    owls,
The owls with their turned heads and everything else that
    is animal.

Then, too, the distant thunder of the garbage truck,
That lumbering urban whale.

Through it all, the mourning doves say
There, there—which is to say, everything is all right.

I believe them. They have said this to me ever since
    childhood.
I hear them. I hear them and I get up.

REFLECTIVE PAUSE

A Welcoming World

It can be useful and centering to meditate on the sounds that begin our days, becoming attuned to certain birdsongs or noises of the human-made world. In "Dawn Callers," Alberto Ríos employs a playfulness with language to convey what brings forth the morning. The speaker describes the calls of birds as "Quick sonic sparks in the morning dark" that help to awaken him. He also hears what's going on around him as "a great tag-of-sounds game," perhaps suggesting that this is a practice for him each morning, waking and naming all of the things and people that "intend themselves to be heard." He invites us to make this a habit for ourselves as well, to sense in the presence of these things that announce themselves each morning a promise that, as the mourning doves suggest, "everything is all right." Rituals like this can provide comfort, especially when our minds run away with overwhelming worry or fear. We might have to look hard in a world that is constantly changing to find such routines, to take solace in what remains the same each day. Yet we can simply pause and return to the moment, allowing the sounds of this world, whether we label them as pleasant or unpleasant, to welcome us back on the path to kindness.

Invitation for Writing and Reflection

Take some time out of the morning to notice the sounds around you that announce the new day. What can you name? What brings you comfort as you listen and identify the source of all those ritual noises?

Susan Moorhead

FIRST LIGHT

I know this sound, first birds of morning.
As a child, I waited for hours for the drape
of night to roll up again. Leaning into the first
hint of the fresh day, the fragile lace of hesitant
light, the receding darkness dappled with bird song,
able at last to close my eyes.

I know this sound, some kind of redemption,
waking me from scattered sleep, a healing fragment
even as the work of the previous day marks my bones
in notches. Night leaves its small fur as the dawn
pushes, as the birds persist, and morning unfurls
like a promise you hoped someone would keep.

Faith Shearin

MY MOTHER'S VAN

Even now it idles outside the houses
where we failed to get better at piano lessons,
visits the parking lot of the ballet school

where my sister and I stood awkwardly
at the back. My mother's van was orange
with a door we slid open to reveal
beheaded plastic dragons and bunches

of black, half-eaten bananas; it was where
her sketchbooks tarried among
abandoned coffee cups and

science projects. She meant to go places
in it: camp in its back seat
and cook on its stove while

painting the coast of Nova Scotia,
or capturing the cold beauty of the Blue Ridge
mountains at dawn. Instead, she waited
behind its wheel while we scraped violins,

made digestive sounds
with trumpets, danced badly at recitals
where grandmothers recorded us

with unsteady cameras. Sometimes, now,
I look out a window and believe I see it,
see her, waiting for me beside a curb,

under a tree, and I think I could open the door,
clear off a seat, look at the drawing in her lap,
which she began, but never seemed to finish.

Ada Limón

THE RAINCOAT

When the doctor suggested surgery
and a brace for all my youngest years,
my parents scrambled to take me
to massage therapy, deep tissue work,
osteopathy, and soon my crooked spine
unspooled a bit, I could breathe again,
and move more in a body unclouded
by pain. My mom would tell me to sing
songs to her the whole forty-five minute
drive to Middle Two Rock Road and forty-
five minutes back from physical therapy.
She'd say, even my voice sounded unfettered
by my spine afterward. So I sang and sang,
because I thought she liked it. I never
asked her what she gave up to drive me,
or how her day was before this chore. Today,
at her age, I was driving myself home from yet
another spine appointment, singing along
to some maudlin but solid song on the radio,
and I saw a mom take her raincoat off
and give it to her young daughter when
a storm took over the afternoon. My god,
I thought, my whole life I've been under her
raincoat thinking it was somehow a marvel
that I never got wet.

Marjorie Saiser

I SAVE MY LOVE

I save my love for what is close,
for the dog's eyes, the depths of brown
when I take a wet cloth to them
to remove the gunk. I save my love
for the smell of coffee at the Mill,
the roasted near-burn of it, especially
the remnant that stays later
in the fibers of my coat. I save my love
for what stays. The white puff
my breath makes when I stand
at night on my doorstep.
That mist doesn't last, gone
like your car turning the corner,
you at the wheel, waving.
Your hand a quick tremble in a
brief illumination. Palm and fingers.
Your face toward me. You had
turned on the overhead light so I would
see you for an instant, see you waving,
see you gone.

Lailah Dainin Shima

IN PRAISE OF DIRTY SOCKS

Say what you want
to stay and never fade.
Choose.

I consider my daughter's socks,
strewn on the sofa. Thick cotton.
Pink with gold-threaded hearts.
Dingy soles. Rank.

Long-ago weeks, when chemo
pinned me like a butterfly,
too nauseous to nag,
she cleaned her things
like saying a spell,
like making a wish.

How she forgets.
How I strain to remember.

How if illness or violence
should still her, the empty arms
of this charcoal couch would ache.

Now the socks draped here
quiet my mind, as morning wind
churns, ferrying amber leaves.

Carolee Bennett

EXACTLY 299,792,458 METERS PER SECOND

On the screen, shadows and bones. My son's
right arm. Radius in two. Displaced. Separated.
In the ER bed, he curls around the misshapen
limb, his skeleton a tiny crescent. Someone's
cranium is projected on the wall in another
room, glaring at us just like the full moon does.
Has it been a skull up above all along? And was
anyone cradling that child until he found his mother?
These questions haunt us, but there is within a secret
glow, exposed by x-ray like a telescope aimed down at
night sky. I don't know where luminosity comes
from, but I've watched a brilliant mechanism
heal the body. Brightness fuses to brightness. Beams
reach for one another across the space between.

Kimberly Blaeser

ABOUT STANDING (IN KINSHIP)

We all have the same little bones in our foot
twenty-six with funny names like *navicular*.
Together they build something strong—
our foot arch a pyramid holding us up.
The bones don't get casts when they break.
We tape them—one *phalange* to its neighbor for support.
(Other things like sorrow work that way, too—
find healing in the leaning, the closeness.)
Our feet have one quarter of all the bones in our body.
Maybe we should give more honor to feet
and to all those tiny but blessed cogs in the world—
communities, the forgotten architecture of friendship.

Rebecca Foust

KINSHIP OF FLESH

I swung my legs up to the table
as I always like to do
and saw another pair
swing up, identical
gesture, length and curve.

I saw your taper-finger,
knot-vein, walnut knuckle
hand just like Mom's
and mine, somehow
knitting together years
miles, dollars, cultures
of division.

Visits, letters, calls, e-mails
dwindled
until it seemed we had less
in common than people I met
on line at the post office.

Then you sat down next me,
sister, and I saw
what I'd forgotten.

Chana Bloch

THE JOINS

Kintsugi is the Japanese art of mending
precious pottery with gold.

What's between us
seems flexible as the webbing
between forefinger and thumb.

Seems flexible but isn't;
what's between us
is made of clay

like any cup on the shelf.
It shatters easily. Repair
becomes the task.

We glue the wounded edges
with tentative fingers.
Scar tissue is visible history

and the cup is precious to us
because
we saved it.

In the art of kintsugi
a potter repairing a broken cup
would sprinkle the resin

with powdered gold.
Sometimes the joins
are so exquisite

they say the potter
may have broken the cup
just so he could mend it.

Heather Swan

BOWL

for my mother

From the mud in her hands,
the bowl was born.
Opening like a flower
in an arch of petals,
then becoming a vessel
both empty and full.

Later, in the kiln
it was ravaged by fire,
its surface etched and vitrified,
searing the glaze into glass
as its body turned
to stone.

It is at the edge of damage
that beauty is honed.
And in Japan,
the potter tells me,
when a tea bowl
cracks in the fire,
that crack is filled
with gold.

REFLECTIVE PAUSE

Where Beauty Is Honed

The practice Heather Swan refers to in the last stanza of "Bowl" is called *kintsugi*, which in Japanese means, literally, "golden joinery." Yet this drive to highlight the cracks in something—what some might call its failures—goes against the message most of us receive throughout our lives, that we should be striving for perfection. We are each born of such humble materials, "From the mud," as it were, and are then sent into the fires of life with little protection, often to be "ravaged . . . etched and vitrified." We are then (oddly enough) encouraged to hide all evidence of past pain, to conceal our scars and the markings that can render us kinder and more compassionate people. Eventually, we come to see, as Swan puts it so well: "It is at the edge of damage that beauty is honed." It is by risking brokenness that we grow stronger, "a vessel both empty and full," made more true by its so-called flaws. Instead of covering up our "cracks" or pretending they don't exist, this poem implies, we can flaunt them like gold for all the world to see.

Invitation for Writing and Reflection

Think back to some supposed flaw or failure in your past, which you have come to see as a source of beauty and strength. How have you learned to highlight your own "cracks," and embrace imperfection as evidence of authenticity and beauty?

Natasha Trethewey

HOUSEKEEPING

We mourn the broken things, chair legs
wrenched from their seats, chipped plates,
the threadbare clothes. We work the magic
of glue, drive the nails, mend the holes.
We save what we can, melt small pieces
of soap, gather fallen pecans, keep neck bones
for soup. Beating rugs against the house,
we watch dust, lit like stars, spreading
across the yard. Late afternoon, we draw
the blinds to cool the rooms, drive the bugs
out. My mother irons, singing, lost in reverie.
I mark the pages of a mail-order catalog,
listen for passing cars. All day we watch
for the mail, some news from a distant place.

Ted Kooser

ROUND ROBIN LETTER

They've all spun down, wobbled, and fallen still
in this digital age, those lost merry-go-rounds
of a whole family's news, each recipient—brother
and sister, cousin or aunt—adding a page or two
written in ballpoint, addressing a fresh envelope,
licking the stamps and mailing it on, plenty of time
between stops to collect something to say, then to
carefully offer it up in school-blackboard cursive—
a nephew who liked his new job, a chestnut foal
born with a diamond-shaped patch on its nose,
a good neighbor who'd been found in his barn
and been buried in rain—each envelope fattened
on gossip and family news, then sent on its way,
an event for the next addressee, something special
to find in the box by the road, then to carry back,
place on the table, and wait, not to be opened
till part of your part of the family was there.

Sally Bliumis-Dunn

MAILMAN

Each day the mailman rides
to a dutiful stop, slides his hand

into the small aluminum tunnel
of our mailbox.

I wonder if the air feels differently
than it did a few years back —
all the emails zipping past him
like no-see-ums.

Sometimes I miss
seeing someone's script

make its way across the envelope
with the sure sense
of the steady straight line,

and then unfolding the letter,
the slight shadows from
the creases as I read it,

reminding me
for a moment of who
had folded and tucked the letter

into the envelope,
sealed it with their tongue,
and carried it to a mailbox

where it sat with all
the other letters in a long silence
that could've lasted for days.

Joseph Millar

TELEPHONE REPAIRMAN

All morning in the February light
he has been mending cable,
splicing the pairs of wires together
according to their colors,
white-blue to white-blue
violet-slate to violet-slate,
in the warehouse attic by the river.
When he is finished
the messages will flow along the line:
thank you for the gift,
please come to the baptism,
the bill is now past due:
voices that flicker and gleam back and forth
across the tracer-colored wires.
We live so much of our lives
without telling anyone,
going out before dawn,
working all day by ourselves,
shaking our heads in silence
at the news on the radio.
He thinks of the many signals
flying in the air around him,
the syllables fluttering,
saying please love me,
from continent to continent
over the curve of the earth.

David Graham

THE NEWS OF LOVE

How old the News of Love must be . . .
—*Emily Dickinson*

The squirrel on our maple flicks
its tail, our dog at his window
watching steadily.

Love is steady, too, and sturdy,
like a thousand year old tree—
they built the house around it.

But dumb love's fun, too,
like the baby laughing nonstop
whenever you rip some paper.

You feel love more than see it,
like the wind on your face.
But don't take my word for it.

Look instead at shoreline pines,
how they all lean one direction,
even when there's no wind.

Linda Hogan

ARCTIC NIGHT, LIGHTS ACROSS THE SKY

We are curved together,
body to body, cell to cell,
arm over another.
The world is the bed for the cold night,
one cat curled in the bend of a knee,
dog at the feet,
my hand in yours, we are embraced
in animal presence, warmth,
the sea outside sounding
winter waves, one arriving after another
from the mystery far out
where in the depths of the sea
are other beings
that create their own light,
this world all one heartbeat.

Alicia Ostriker

THE DOGS AT LIVE OAK BEACH, SANTA CRUZ

As if there could be a world
Of absolute innocence
In which we forget ourselves

The owners throw sticks
And half-bald tennis balls
Toward the surf
And the happy dogs leap after them
As if catapulted—

Black dogs, tan dogs,
Tubes of glorious muscle—

Pursuing pleasure
More than obedience
They race, skid to a halt in the wet sand,
Sometimes they'll plunge straight into
The foaming breakers

Like diving birds, letting the green turbulence
Toss them, until they snap and sink

Teeth into floating wood
Then bound back to their owners
Shining wet, with passionate speed
For nothing,
For absolutely nothing but joy.

Nancy Gordon

RESCUE DOG

Jake comes into sight—ten pounds
of whirling golden fur, legs and feet a blur,
released from his leash to greet me,
racing toward me.
Eyes dark pools, shining, ears flapping
with his running and jumping—
up into my arms, onto my shoulder,
his body close to my chest—my heart.
Tongue lapping everywhere—"doggy kisses,"
says my friend who lets me share walks with him.
Quick breaths, his heart pounding, his body
warm and flexible as a gymnast's.

He drinks water from my hands.
He walks us. He explores the scents, the grass,
all that he can reach from his reattached leash.
He and my friend debate the boundaries.

When I have to leave, I turn to watch them go.
And Jake turns, looks back, looks back again,
crooks his head—
where are you going? aren't you coming with us?

Dan Butler

NEW YORK DOWNPOUR

The night sky cracked open on us full force,
a deluge, a drench, and laughing, arms around
one another, we soaked it up like a couple
of Gene Kellys, stomping, singing, not even
a twinge of an urge to run, just pure revel,
hummingbird joy, as lightning flashed
capturing the moment. Soon the storm
grew tired of scaring us off the streets
and subsided into grumpy rumblings,
while we splashed our way through puddles
from West End Avenue through Riverside Park
all the way to the edge of the Hudson.

Richard Jones

AFTER WORK

Coming up from the subway
into the cool Manhattan evening,
I feel rough hands on my heart—
women in the market yelling
over rows of tomatoes and peppers,
old men sitting on a stoop playing cards,
cabbies cursing each other with fists
while the music of church bells
sails over the street,
and the father, angry and tired
after working all day,
embracing his little girl,
kissing her,
mi vida, mi corazón,
brushing the hair out of her eyes
so she can see.

ABUNDANCE TO SHARE WITH THE BIRDS

Another early morning
in front of the bathroom mirror—
my daughter making faces
at herself while I pull
back her long brown hair,
gathering the breadth and shine
in my hands, brushing
and smoothing before weaving
the braid she will wear
to school for the day.
Afterwards, stray strands
nestle in the brush, and because
nothing of beauty is ever wasted,
I pull them out,
stand on the front porch and let them fly.

Fady Joudah

MIMESIS

My daughter
                    wouldn't hurt a spider
That had nested
Between her bicycle handles
For two weeks
She waited
Until it left of its own accord

If you tear down the web I said
It will simply know
This isn't a place to call home
And you'd get to go biking

She said that's how others
Become refugees isn't it?

Rudy Francisco

MERCY

after Nikki Giovanni

She asks me to kill the spider.
Instead, I get the most
peaceful weapons I can find.

I take a cup and a napkin.
I catch the spider, put it outside
and allow it to walk away.

If I am ever caught in the wrong place
at the wrong time, just being alive
and not bothering anyone,

I hope I am greeted
with the same kind
of mercy.

Naomi Shihab Nye

KINDNESS

Before you know what kindness really is
you must lose things,
feel the future dissolve in a moment
like salt in a weakened broth.
What you held in your hand,
what you counted and carefully saved,
all this must go so you know
how desolate the landscape can be
between the regions of kindness.
How you ride and ride
thinking the bus will never stop,
the passengers eating maize and chicken
will stare out the window forever.

Before you learn the tender gravity of kindness,
you must travel where the Indian in a white poncho
lies dead by the side of the road.
You must see how this could be you,
how he too was someone
who journeyed through the night with plans
and the simple breath that kept him alive.

Before you know kindness as the deepest thing inside,
you must know sorrow as the other deepest thing.
You must wake up with sorrow.
You must speak to it till your voice
catches the thread of all sorrows

and you see the size of the cloth.
Then it is only kindness that makes sense anymore,
only kindness that ties your shoes
and sends you out into the day to mail letters and purchase
     bread,
only kindness that raises its head
from the crowd of the world to say
it is I you have been looking for,
and then goes with you everywhere
like a shadow or a friend.

Christine Kitano

FOR THE KOREAN GRANDMOTHER ON
SUNSET BOULEVARD

So you are here. Night comes as it does
elsewhere: light pulls slowly away
from telephone posts, shadows of buildings
darken the pavement like something
spilled. Even the broken moon
seems to turn its face.
And again you find yourself
on this dark riverbed, this asphalt
miracle, holding your end of a rope
that goes slack when you tug it.
Such grief you bear alone.
But wait. Just now a light
approaches, its rich band draws
you forward, out of shadow.
It is here, the bus that will ferry
you home. Go ahead,
grandmother, go on.

REFLECTIVE PAUSE

So You Are Here

As Christine Kitano shows in her moving poem, if we're present enough to another person, we can sometimes become attuned to what they're feeling. In fact, even the act of paying attention to a stranger can create a sense of connection, no matter how fleeting. The speaker in this poem watches the Korean grandmother at a bus stop so closely that she seems to feel her way into the grief that this older woman must bear alone. Yet that sadness soon lifts as "a light approaches" and "its rich band draws you forward, out of shadow." Both strangers seem brought out of the shadows by their momentary brush with each other, reminding me of what June Jordan once wrote: "I am a stranger learning to worship the strangers around me." If we can learn to see even the people we don't know in our lives as worthy of reverence and attention, perhaps we can treat ourselves with that same kindness and regard. Ultimately, this poem serves as a blessing for the grandmother who, through the act of the speaker's close observation, becomes a stranger no longer.

Invitation for Writing and Reflection

Have you had a moment like the one Christine Kitano describes here, of almost being able to see into someone else's life? See if you can re-create that moment and capture the connection you felt.

Paula Gordon Lepp

GAS STATION COMMUNION

It was a little thing, really,
this offer to fill my tire.
I was unscrewing the valve cap
and heard a voice behind me,
"Here, I'll get that for you."

"Oh that's okay, I've got it," is what
I normally say to such overtures,
this knee-jerk reaction to refuse.
I am the one who offers to help,
I am the one who serves.

Perhaps it was the eager spirit
in his face or his brown eyes
full of hopeful connection that
caused me to say okay.

I felt the vibration of
his unspoken benediction:
I can't do much for you,
fellow weary traveler,
but I can do this. Lay
down your burden and
I will carry it for a bit.

And I couldn't help but wonder
how many times I have denied
someone the blessing of serving

because I have been too stubborn
to accept their gift.

As I was standing there
in the sun-drenched gas station
parking lot, the hiss and tick of
the air pump sounded very much
like a psalm. I watched his hands
filling more than just my tire with air,
while goodness and grace
swirled around us.

Annie Lighthart

A GREAT WILD GOODNESS

One morning I was looking out the window
when a great wild goodness came over me:
I wanted to be kind to everything. I promised
not to kill the big spider on the wall; in the cold
I took the dog for the long walk she'd been wanting;
I fetched a trash can lid for an ornery neighbor
and did not, just then, add a single adjective to his name.
I went back inside to the laundry and dishes
with a clean heart such as I have never had.

Before dinner the wild goodness shouted, "Too tame!
Too tame!" so I went outside without my coat
and shouted poems up to the stars
until my children came home with their small
warm hands. Then we ate bread
in the kitchen, unafraid to be happy.
The stars in wild darkness were right over our heads.

Ellen Rowland

NO SMALL THING

The smell of baking bread, smooth floured hands,
butter waiting to be spread with blackberry jam
and I realize, this is no small thing.
These days spent confined,
I am drawn to life's ordinary details,
the largeness of all we can do
alongside what we cannot.
The list of allowances far outweighs my complaints.
I am fortunate to have flour and yeast, a source of heat
not to mention soft butter, the tartness of blackberries
harvested on a cold back road.
A kitchen, a home, two working
hands to stir and knead,
a clear enough head to gather it all.
Even the big toothy knife feels miraculous
as it grabs hold and cracks the crust.

Jane Hirshfield

I WOULD LIKE

I would like
my living to inhabit me
the way
rain, sun, and their wanting
inhabit a fig or apple.

I would like to meet it
also in pieces,
scattered:
a conversation set down
on a long hallway table;

a disappointment
pocketed inside a jacket;
some long-ago longing glimpsed,
half-recognized,
in the corner of a thrift store painting.

To discover my happiness,
walking first
toward
then away from me
down a stairwell,
on two strong legs all its own.

Also,
the uncountable
wheat stalks,

how many times broken,
beaten, sent
between grindstones,
before entering
the marriage
of oven and bread—

Let me find my life in that, too.

In my moments
of clumsiness, solitude;
in days of vertigo and hesitation;
in the many year-ends
that found me
standing on top of a stovetop
to take down a track light.

In my nights' asked,
sometimes answered, questions.

I would like
to add to my life,
while we are still living,
a little salt and butter,
one more slice of the edible apple,
a teaspoon of jam
from the long-simmered fig.

To taste
as if something tasted for the first time
what we will have become then.

Peter Pereira

A POT OF RED LENTILS

simmers on the kitchen stove.
All afternoon dense kernels
surrender to the fertile
juices, their tender bellies
swelling with delight.

In the yard we plant
rhubarb, cauliflower, and artichokes,
cupping wet earth over tubers,
our labor the germ
of later sustenance and renewal.

Across the field the sound of a baby crying
as we carry in the last carrots,
whorls of butter lettuce,
a basket of red potatoes.

I want to remember us this way—
late September sun streaming through
the window, bread loaves and golden
bunches of grapes on the table,
spoonfuls of hot soup rising
to our lips, filling us
with what endures.

William Stafford

YOU READING THIS, BE READY

Starting here, what do you want to remember?
How sunlight creeps along a shining floor?
What scent of old wood hovers, what softened
sound from outside fills the air?

Will you ever bring a better gift for the world
than the breathing respect that you carry
wherever you go right now? Are you waiting
for time to show you some better thoughts?

When you turn around, starting here, lift this
new glimpse that you found; carry into evening
all that you want from this day. This interval you spent
reading or hearing this, keep it for life—

What can anyone give you greater than now,
starting here, right in this room, when you turn around?

Connie Wanek

COME IN!

for Marsha

It was the neighbor at the back door
with a Vidalia onion in each hand,
straight from the ten-pound sack
the Shriners were selling, or the Rotarians
or Odd Fellows or one of those
antique civic organizations of great uncles
atoning for their sins on a just-in-time basis.

"Come in!" And she did, smiling.
The fifteen months of Covid had given
those simple words a radical new meaning,
an assertiveness. I felt I was
tearing up a contract I never wanted to sign,
membership in an HOA maybe.

Pale yellow onions, too clean
to have come from the soil, surely,
too sweet to make you cry.

Susan Rich

STILL LIFE WITH LADDER

Today, the sky saved my life
caught between smoked rum and cornflower.
Today, there is a color I can't name cruising past

the backdoor—it is the idea of color.
Cloudscapes evaporate like love songs
across lost islands, each a small bitcoin of thought.

Today, I am alive and this is a good thing—

clams in the half shell, a lemon rosemary tart.
I live in the day and the day lives past me.
If I could draw a map of the hours, a long

horizon would travel on indefinitely—a green, backlit
      thread.

The sky? It is never the same—it is sour milk
and whipped cream, a sketchbook and flour-dusted jeans.
Today, I am in love with the sky.

It doesn't care if my father is dead,
or that I live by myself with his Masonic watch.
I sew time with my mother's button jar.

I've improvised my life —let the sky pull the strings.

Tonight, I will borrow the golden ladder from the orchard,
travel from this sphere into the next and expunge
the leftover sadness of the hemispheres, to move beyond

the beyond which is here, present, alive in this hyacinth
      room;

time leaps over itself, after and out of the tangled past
over shadows of weather falling across a back window—
to forgive one another; to try once more to live it right.

Alison Luterman

BRAIDING HIS HAIR

Here we are each morning:
my husband on our old kitchen chair, its upholstery
mended with duct tape, his head bent forward
while I comb out his long
wheat-colored hair. Not what I thought
we'd be doing in our sixties,
me dividing the wet silk of it, still stubbornly
reddish-gold, only a little
white at the sideburns. Three thick hanks
in hand, I begin to plait: *over, under, over, under.*
I don't remember when he stopped
cutting his hair and decided
to let it grow long as a girl's —
and he was mistaken for a girl once,
a tall, stoop-shouldered man-girl,
when he stood on the sidewalk, back to the street,
and a car drove by, honking and catcalling.
At him, not me. We laughed,
but I had to wonder: When did his tresses, now
halfway to his waist, first spill
over his shoulders? It must have happened while we slept,
as most things do. And how did he come to sit
before me so patiently now, head bowed while I braid,
as if he were the daughter I never had
and this my one chance
to weave my care into each *over, under,*
over, under?

Judith Sornberger

LOVE IN OUR SIXTIES

For Karl

You lead me, hand in hand,
through your apple orchard
like the one where I was
married half a life ago.
Although we met when old,
I once thought we might wed,
become partners as we were
with our former, longtime loves.

You're showing me the once-wild
apple tree onto whose boughs
you grafted other varieties—
Priscilla, Fameuse, Ida Red—
like the names of children
we will never have.

I once hoped that we—potter
and poet, man and woman—
might graft our lives in such a way
that they couldn't be divided,
though we're as white-haired
as crowns of apple trees in May.

You point out the raised place
where old met new and melded
right down to the heartwood,

where separateness has almost
been erased. I trace the scar
as you reach up to pick a few
apples for us to taste.
Oh, the scarlet kiss of skin,
the sweetness of today.

Susan Rothbard

THAT NEW

At the market today, I look for Piñata
apples, their soft-blush-yellow. My husband
brought them home last week, made me guess at
the name of this new strain, held one in his hand
like a gift and laughed as I tried all
the names I knew: Gala, Fuji, Honey
Crisp—watched his face for clues—what to call
something new? It's winter, only tawny
hues and frozen ground, but that apple bride
was sweet, and I want to bring it back to him,
that new. When he cut it, the star inside
held seeds of other stars, the way within
a life are all the lives you might live,
each unnamed, until you name it.

Susan Zimmerman

GET CLOSE

So close you see something you thought you knew
as if for the first time, then closer, beyond seeing—
lost, mystified.

Like the time I photographed
the grey shadow on the side of a tree, magnifying
until I realized it was not a shadow but growing moss.

Until I realized the white dots were not dots
but tiny flowers blooming in the moss,
until I was so close I disappeared.

In the whole universe there was nothing
and no one but the tree and me,
and we were only one thing.

David Axelrod

THE INNERMOST CHAMBER OF MY
HOME IS YOURS

Until now, I hadn't looked up all day—

it's already late October
and this last month of the campaign
the rains returned,

the Earth soft underfoot,
lawns in town, fescue, wildrye
and bunchgrass in the foothills,
winter wheat in the valley,

all bled together into a green film.

And for no reason at all
I glanced up the slopes
at Glass Hill, where forests
burned forty years ago

and caught a glimpse of it—
a future world
where a young aspen grove

yields back all of summer's light into air.

Dave Baldwin

SUMMER ROMANCE

Of all my days to middle age,
you gave me less than ten;
so little time

from moon to rising moon.
A meteor flared and fell
on an August night

now thirty winters dead.
The lingering light:
for that, I give you thanks.

Anya Silver

LATE SUMMER

August evening, church bells,
light shattered on the quick
creek as in a Seurat painting,
grass thick with Queen Anne's lace,
the summer sun still so late
in setting that bedtime comes late
for the children scattered in a garden
to catch the slugs eating their plants.
Late summer, and the roses in second
bloom know what's coming.
But for now, bells, water, laughter,
my mother and I walking together
arm in arm, because happiness
is a decision each of us has made,
without even discussing it.

Judith Sornberger

ASSISTED LIVING

This time, Mom, I'd stay overnight
at Assisted Living when you asked.
Borrow a pair of your satin pajamas,
paint your fingernails pearly white.
Finish off a box of Russell Stover
chocolates with you. I wouldn't
even complain when you pinched
each piece to reveal its center,
avoiding the dreaded marshmallow.

Forgive me. I was trying to avoid
sleeping on the sofa too narrow
for my body, staying up later
than I like while you filled ashtrays
with cigarette butts and my eyes
burned and watered from your smoke.

This time I'd visit the past
for as long as you wanted.
Sit with you, hip to hip,
looking at pictures of me
and my sisters, the ones with
scalloped white edges like
the lace on our Easter anklets.
I'd watch as many classic black
and white flicks as you wished,
and weep beside you at their endings.

Patricia McKernon Runkle

WHEN YOU MEET SOMEONE DEEP IN GRIEF

Slip off your needs
and set them by the door.

Enter barefoot
this darkened chapel

hollowed by loss
hallowed by sorrow

its gray stone walls
and floor.

You, congregation
of one

are here to listen
not to sing.

Kneel in the back pew.
Make no sound,

let the candles
speak.

REFLECTIVE PAUSE

Here to Listen

Patricia McKernon Runkle's words call us to be as present as possible with another person, to recognize the sanctity of the space we share with someone who has recently endured a loss of any kind. She asks us to see the "hollowing" of grief as a "hallowing" as well, deserving of reverence. With its short lines and many pauses, the poem makes us feel as if we too are entering the "darkened chapel," step by slow step, toward the person who needs us, and she reminds us, most importantly, that we are "here to listen not to sing." When sitting with someone in mourning, we might think it's our job to fix things for them, to make the other person feel better. Yet often what we most need from a companion is their deep presence, their willingness to enter the place of mystery, confusion, and pain with us. That's the greatest gift we can give to another during a trying time, and it's essential to point out that Runkle's poem also works in another way: We can just as easily take her advice when we meet *ourselves* in the depths of loss. At that time too, all we can do is listen deeply to the self and its needs, leaving all expectations for outcome or a quick recovery at the door.

Invitation for Writing and Reflection

Is there a time when someone showed up for you, or you showed up for someone else during a difficult loss in their lives? How were you able to offer compassion, and how were you changed by that experience?

Megan Buchanan

DREAM VISITATION

This morning before dawn,
my dad visited me in my dream.
He was here, where I live now
in a house he never did see.
I came down the wide staircase
with a lost dog
that had spent the night,
to find my dad
sitting in a chair near the kitchen.

As I walked into the lamp-lit room,
he rose up and hugged me.
He was wearing a red plaid shirt
and his navy blue blazer,
signifying important business.
He was warm; it was him.
He held me tightly in his arms,
my tears streamed.

With a gasp, I asked, *Dad!*
Where are you now? Where did you go?
And he answered:
I am in the pixels
of the pictures you are looking at
by which I think he meant:
I am here
and everywhere.

Phyllis Cole-Dai

LADDER

for my father

The night before you died
I dreamed a wooden ladder
rose straight into the sky,
propped against only a wall of air
yet sturdy on its feet, like you
in that faded old photo, tall and lean,
knee-high in a field of ripening beans.

I wasn't with you at the end
but I know that when you left your bed
you mounted that ladder, young again,
body light and nimble, clambering up
the rungs worn smooth by shoes
and stained from use like wooden spoons.
After a few uncertain steps,
your long legs took them two at a time,
a rapturous climb to glory,
up past the crowns of maples and oaks,
up past the tops of barns and silos,
up past the soaring vultures and hawks,
up through the thin cool veil of clouds.
Now and then on your way to the stars
I see you pause upon that ladder,
look down from the heavens,

not to gauge how far you've come
but to gaze with love on what you loved.

Michelle Mandolia

THE THING SHE LOVES MOST

I hear my daughter introduce
her favorite stuffed animal to her kindergarten class.
The school year is more than half over
and she has spent it in this house
peering into this one screen.
Her first name is Reeree, I hear my daughter say,
*and her last name is Hillary. She doesn't have a middle
     name.*
I picture the audience, squares on her screen,
her teacher's broad smile of interest, the alert posture
of the boy who signs in first every morning,
the foreheads of children looking down to doodle,
as my daughter often does, the unoccupied desk
of someone who is using the potty.
These five and six year olds have met Reeree
at least ten times, maybe twenty.
I am grateful for whatever instructional philosophy
keeps the teacher from suggesting a new share.
On these days, my daughter gets a few extra moments
with the thing she loves most.
Her turn over, her fingertips skim Reeree's coat, settling
on the mane, felted from so much washing.

Marjorie Saiser

LAST DAY OF KINDERGARTEN

In the photograph
the boy is ecstatic,
set free, a young king,
everything ahead of him.
There is nothing he can't have
if he wants it and he wants it,
as does his friend beside him.
They are ready now to ride off
together and slay dragons,
rescue the world. It's all here
in the park after the last bell;
it's here in the green summer
they have been released to.
It's here in their manhood.
They've only finished kindergarten
but they understand freedom
and friendship. They're on top
of the picnic table, they're on top
of the world in their tennis shoes,
they have raised their arms,
they are such men as could
raise continents; they have
survived. Look how their
fingers reach the sky

and their legs are sure as
horses. Their bodies
will forever do anything they ask.

Gillian Wegener

JUVIE KID

for Gus

Again, we meet in the hallway.
As usual, he's sweeping the floor.

Look at all the bugs, he says, leaning in
to examine his pile of dust and flies.

Hey, he says, *when are you going
to write poetry with us?*

His hair a wild halo, his eyes intense,
his shoulders not yet as wide as mine.

He means, when will I matter to you?

I've been in here four whole months,
he says. *But I'm getting out soon.*

I'm going to a group home, far away.
They gave me a choice, but I don't care where.

Far away from here.

Regulations say no handshakes, no touching.
We aren't supposed to be talking, but

we say good luck, good luck. We say
something about second chances
something about taking the right path.

We aren't supposed to be talking to him,
this boy, excited at what's ahead.

We turn and pause at another door.
We know his slim chances.

Pray for me, he calls. *Pray for me, okay?*

Emilie Lygren

MAKE BELIEVE

Mr. Rogers, what would you say to us now?
I miss your soft voice and slow smile.

Somehow you would remind us of what it means to share a
    neighborhood—
how our breath travels farther than we think,
but so can our care.

You would've made the puppets tiny cloth masks,
had them ask all the questions children need to ask like,
Why? and *How Long?* and *Can't we ... ?*
Let Daniel Tiger feel sad and antsy, itchy under the ear
    straps.

You would have explained it all patiently and truthfully:
    No, we don't know how long.
    Yes, it's OK to feel afraid.
    This is how we care for everyone right now.

Maybe the adults would have listened, too.

Brad Aaron Modlin

WHAT YOU MISSED THAT DAY YOU WERE
ABSENT FROM FOURTH GRADE

Mrs. Nelson explained how to stand still and listen
to the wind, how to find meaning in pumping gas,

how peeling potatoes can be a form of prayer. She took
questions on how not to feel lost in the dark

After lunch she distributed worksheets
that covered ways to remember your grandfather's

voice. Then the class discussed falling asleep
without feeling you had forgotten to do something else—

something important—and how to believe
the house you wake in is your home. This prompted

Mrs. Nelson to draw a chalkboard diagram detailing
how to chant the Psalms during cigarette breaks,

and how not to squirm for sound when your own thoughts
are all you hear; also, that you have enough.

The English lesson was that *I am*
is a complete sentence.

And just before the afternoon bell, she made the math
     equation
look easy. The one that proves that hundreds of questions,

and feeling cold, and all those nights spent looking
for whatever it was you lost, and one person

add up to something.

What You Missed

At times, we might feel that we missed out on some necessary information for life handed out to everyone else long ago. It's a natural human response to compare ourselves to others, to look around and wonder why they seem to have it together, possessing some secret knowledge that we don't. Brad Aaron Modlin offers a playful yet sincere take on this idea as he explores what we all might have missed that day in fourth grade when we were absent, unraveling a list of the kinder, wiser things we might wish our teachers would have taught us. It could have been useful, for instance, to be told that "*I am* is a complete sentence," to stop feeling that we have to be someone other than who we are to feel worthy. Or we might have been shown "how to find meaning in pumping gas," or turn an act as ordinary as peeling potatoes into "a form of prayer." This poem longs for some deeper knowledge that would have matched the tender needs of a child, like "worksheets that covered ways to remember your grandfather's voice," or "how to believe the house you wake in is your home." Perhaps we might all have felt more at home if we had been given the freedom and kindness as kids simply to be ourselves.

Invitation for Writing and Reflection

What do you wish your teachers and grown-ups would have taught you? And what might be more helpful to know now in everyday life? Feel free to be both playful and profound as you work with this idea.

Dorianne Laux

ON THE BACK PORCH

The cat calls for her dinner.
On the porch I bend and pour
brown soy stars into her bowl,
stroke her dark fur.
It's not quite night.
Pinpricks of light in the eastern sky.
Above my neighbor's roof, a transparent
moon, a pink rag of cloud.
Inside my house are those who love me.
My daughter dusts biscuit dough.
And there's a man who will lift my hair
in his hands, brush it
until it throws sparks.
Everything is just as I've left it.
Dinner simmers on the stove.
Glass bowls wait to be filled
with gold broth. Sprigs of parsley
on the cutting board.
I want to smell this rich soup, the air
around me going dark, as stars press
their simple shapes into the sky.
I want to stay on the back porch
while the world tilts
toward sleep, until what I love
misses me, and calls me in.

Suzanne Nussey

LULLABY FOR AN EMPTY NESTER

You have a bed that loves your bones.
The dog snores softly at your feet,
partnering your partner's drone.
Hermit thrush and tree frog sing
the creeping dark to sleep.
Make a cradle of the night,
a cradle for what's gone.
Nothing to fear
in your twilight.
You are here.
You are home.

Michelle Wiegers

MOVING

I find myself jealous of those who rest
quarantined inside their homes,
while I have to pack every last item I own
in order to carry it just a few blocks away.

And now as I reach around inside
this new house, I keep looking
for the things I know, certainties to hold
me up, cushion me on all sides.

How do I know that all will be well?

Because the morning sun still
warms my cheek, illuminating
small flecks of dust on my glasses
that look like layered circles of modern art.

Because the red squirrel still comes to raid
the feeders I hang, not intended for him
while the chickadee sings
his same vibrant song.

Because the ferns in my garden
I feared had not survived the move
are finally unfurling
their bright green bodies.

Because spring doesn't know
the anxiety of uncertainty,
but declares, through her gentle unwrapping
of the world, life will come again.

Marie Howe

DELIVERY

The delivery man slowly climbs
the five steep flights of stairs
as I lean down to watch him walking up

as he's talking on the phone
and now he pauses
on the third-floor landing

to touch a little Christmas light
the girl had wrapped around the banister—
speaking to someone in a language
so melodic I ask him what—
when he hands the package up to me,
and he says Patois—from Jamaica—
smiling up at me from where he's standing
on the landing

a smile so radiant that
re-entering the apartment I'm
a young woman again, and
the sweetness of the men I've loved walks in,
through the closed door

one of them right now,
kicking the snow off his boots,
turning to take my face in his cold hands,
kissing me now with his cold mouth.

Ray Hudson

UNBREAKABLE CLARITIES

Across America
curtains are pulled open
and delivery trucks back up
ever so carefully with the sun

in their rearview mirrors.
The coffee is almost
ready. On a pad beside
the telephone is the number

you left when you called.
It is too early to call you back
and to tell you how
it began snowing

last night after I had gone
to bed and how
outside, beneath the window,
a few leaves are still green

and how the barbed wire
between me and the field
glistens with frost.
I am blinded by unfamiliar

possibilities. I count myself
lucky to live in such times
as I hit the replay button
just to hear your voice.

Danusha Laméris

INSHA'ALLAH

I don't know when it slipped into my speech
that soft word meaning, "if God wills it."
Insha'Allah I will see you next summer.
The baby will come in spring insha'Allah.
Insha'Allah this year we will have enough rain.

So many plans I've laid have unraveled
easily as braids beneath my mother's quick fingers.

Every language must have a word for this. A word
our grandmothers uttered under their breath
as they pinned the whites, soaked in lemon,
hung them to dry in the sun, or peeled potatoes,
dropping the discarded skins into a bowl.

Our sons will return next month, insha'Allah.
Insha'Allah this war will end, soon. Insha'Allah
the rice will be enough to last through the winter.

How lightly we learn to hold hope,
as if it were an animal that could turn around
and bite your hand. And still we carry it
the way a mother would, carefully,
from one day to the next.

Andrea Potos

WHERE I MIGHT FIND HER

for Mom

Overnight it seems, the pink vaults
of the peonies open;
in an iridescent second, a hummingbird
twirls inches from my face.

Pennies spot the sidewalk—so bright,
I believe they would smile if they could.

And if kindness were air, the rooms of my house
expand with it.
Breathing deeply is simple, and hope
is the natural choice.

Rosemerry Wahtola Trommer

THE QUESTION

for Jude Janett

All day, I replay these words:
Is this the path of love?
I think of them as I rise, as
I wake my children, as I wash dishes,
as I drive too close behind the slow
blue Subaru, *Is this the path of love?*
Think of them as I stand in line
at the grocery store,
think of them as I sit on the couch
with my daughter. Amazing how
quickly six words become compass,
the new lens through which to see myself
in the world. I notice what the question is not.
Not, "Is this right?" Not,
"Is this wrong?" It just longs to know
how the action of existence
links us to the path to love.
And is it *this*? Is it *this*? All day
I let myself be led by the question.
All day I let myself not be too certain
of the answer. *Is it this?* I ask as I
argue with my son. *Is it this?* I ask
as I wait for the next word to come.

Jacqueline Suskin

FUTURE

I can't see my future clearly.
It's a wash of color and light.
Maybe a glimpse of a house
with wood floors, the death
of a parent, a dog, a cat, a love,
but nothing certain. I like its fog.
Inevitably something will happen, pieces
will fall into place if I keep breathing
and I'll eat, I'll work, I'll learn
and know and forget. There'll be
another bowl full of berries, a hot cup
of tea, additional travel and sorrow.
There'll be a clean pair of pants,
the sun's good glow, a cut and blood,
a hole to dig, a bath to take, a mistake to mend.
What lies ahead is a promise
standing in shadow, one second
pasted to the next. I don't need to call it
by name. A riddle ensues, a song of guessing,
a vow of risk. The road becomes itself
single stone after single stone
made of limitless possibility,
endless awe.

READING GROUP QUESTIONS AND TOPICS FOR DISCUSSION

"Small Kindnesses" by Danusha Laméris (Page 5)

- How would you define *kindness*? What does the word mean to you?

- In this poem, Laméris meditates on all the small ways we take care of each other, pointing out: "Mostly, we don't want to harm each other." Do you agree that kindness is our basic nature as humans?

- The speaker wonders if the "moments of exchange" between us are the "true dwelling of the holy," yet goes on to call them "fleeting temples." Why do you think negative experiences often stay with us longer than the positive? How might we train ourselves to hold on to kindness and joy?

- **INVITATION FOR WRITING AND REFLECTION:** Write a list of the small kindnesses you have received or given recently, those "moments of exchange" that we might ignore or take for granted. You might also make this a regular part of your writing practice, keeping a kindness journal to capture such moments of connection.

"Elation" by January Gill O'Neil (Page 19)

- We forget how deeply we can connect with the natural world when we make the time to go outside. How does this poem make these "Tolerant trees" come more alive for the reader?

- The next time you happen to be among trees, listen to the sounds they make in the wind. The speaker here describes them as being like "rocking chairs," "a cello's drawn breath," and "the chatter between old, coupled voices." How would you describe that sound yourself?
- Why does the speaker come to see these trees as such resilient beings? What lessons might we humans learn from the trees?
- INVITATION FOR WRITING AND REFLECTION: Think back to a time when you had a similar sense of "elation" while in nature. What did you notice that you had never paid attention to before?

"Coniferous Fathers" by Michael Kleber-Diggs
(Page 82)

- How does Michael Kleber-Diggs challenge our typical ideas about how fathers and men in general should behave?
- Why do you think he chose the metaphor of "coniferous" trees like pines to describe the kind of father he would prefer, "soft enough to bend"?
- How does this poem imagine a new type of intimacy between fathers and their children? What images of connection stand out to you?
- INVITATION FOR WRITING AND REFLECTION: Write a wish list for your own ideal father. What qualities would he embody for you, and what images spring to mind as you consider those perhaps more loving, gentler, and softer traits?

"Mimesis" by Fady Joudah (Page 125)

- Young people have the uncanny ability to distill what we believe are complex concepts into the simplest, most relatable human terms. How does the speaker's daughter help him to understand the plight of refugees more clearly?

- Why is the daughter's argument for kindness so moving and convincing?

- How is the father's initial justification for destroying the spider's home similar to justifications we often hear from governments, including our own, especially during times of war?

- INVITATION FOR WRITING AND REFLECTION: What living things in your own daily life do you often look past or brush away, which you might work to include more fully in your own sense of compassion and empathy?

"The Raincoat" by Ada Limón (Page 103)

- What kinds of sacrifices do the speaker's parents make in this poem to correct her "crooked spine," and to help her finally "breathe again"?

- What do you think of the speaker's revelation when she says of her mother, "I never asked her what she gave up to drive me." What do you think she means in that final image when she realizes she's been "under her raincoat" for her whole life?

- Do you see similarities between Ada Limón's poem and "My Mother's Van" by Faith Shearin (page 101), both of which focus on the sacrifice of mothers? How have those sacrifices followed each of these speakers into their present lives?

- INVITATION FOR WRITING AND REFLECTION: Think about a time when a parental figure or mentor made sacrifices for your well-being. Did you recognize what they were doing for you and what they were giving up at the time? How did those past sacrifices help you to become who you are?

"About Standing (in Kinship)" by Kimberly Blaeser
(Page 107)

- This poem begins with one way we are similar as humans: "We all have the same little bones in our foot." How does the poet use this image to capture the idea of community and connection among us?

- When she discusses how we tape together broken toes for support and healing, she points out that "Other things like sorrow work that way, too." What are the ways we can "find healing in the leaning, the closeness," especially when someone is struggling?

- Why does the poet suggest we ought to "give more honor to feet," even going so far as to call them "blessed cogs in the world"? What are some other "blessed cogs" we might work to honor in our lives and society?

- INVITATION FOR WRITING AND REFLECTION: Think back to a time when you found "healing in the leaning, the closeness," and reached out to others for help with a difficult situation. How did you manage to move beyond your isolation, and remember the "kinship" that allows us all to thrive?

"Kinship of Flesh" by Rebecca Foust (Page 108)

- When we disagree fundamentally with others, it can be easy to forget their humanity. How does this poem call us back to our essential connection with each other, especially with other family members?

- What allows the speaker of this poem to see what she had forgotten about how "knitt[ed] together" she is with her sister?

- What do you make of the title of the poem, especially the word *kinship*? How does Foust encourage us to see ourselves in others from whom we feel so separate?

- **INVITATION FOR WRITING AND REFLECTION:** Describe a time when you were able to see and feel your way past a disagreement or division with someone else. What brought you back to the fact of your connectedness? How can you practice seeing the humanity and kinship in others who seem so different from you?

"Filling the Candles" by Ted Kooser (Page 25)

- How does the speaker's close observation of the church volunteer who has come to fill the candles bring "a little warmth" to this otherwise chilly day?
- Shared ritual and routine often steady us during challenging times and give us a sense of purpose. Based on Kooser's intricate descriptions of this woman, how would you describe her devotion to this act? Do you think she finds pleasure in what she's doing?
- How does the woman filling the candles, and the speaker who's watching her, encourage us to bring mindfulness and deep attention to the seemingly ordinary acts of our lives?
- **INVITATION FOR WRITING AND REFLECTION:** Consider some ritual that's become an important part of your life. What do you do to fulfill this task, paying close attention to every detail, as the poet does here? How does this routine ground you in the moment and connect you with others?

"Late Summer" by Anya Silver (Page 149)

- How does the poet capture the beauty and joy of a late summer evening? What sensory details stand out to you?
- What do you think Silver means when she says, "the roses in second bloom know what's coming," given the fact that autumn is just around the corner?

- In the final lines of the poem, we see the speaker and her mother, "walking together arm in arm, because happiness is a decision each of us has made." Do you feel that happiness is a choice or decision we can each make, no matter the circumstances?
- INVITATION FOR WRITING AND REFLECTION: Was there a time when you felt yourself immersed in the joy of a moment that you knew would end but that you decided to savor anyway? What images come back from that time, and what makes them so vivid to you?

"On the Back Porch" by Dorianne Laux (Page 165)

- The speaker re-creates a moment of joy and completeness that might seem plain to some. As she stands out on her back porch, how does she convey the gratefulness she feels for this simple moment when, as she says, "Inside my house are those who love me"?
- How do Dorianne Laux's word choices ("sparks," "gold," and "rich") affect the way we read this poem? What are some of the concrete descriptions that bring us into the scene?
- She ends by saying, "I want to stay on the back porch . . . until what I love misses me, and calls me in." Why is it necessary for us to step out of our lives in order to fully appreciate what we have right now?
- INVITATION FOR WRITING AND REFLECTION: As you move through the next few days, stay on the lookout for moments of sudden connection and joy, and see if you can drop into them fully. With a notebook, or just in your mind, pause and take stock of what's around you. What calls to you as you savor the gift of the moment?

POET BIOGRAPHIES

Kelli Russell Agodon's fourth collection of poems, *Dialogues with Rising Tides,* was published by Copper Canyon Press. She's the cofounder of Two Sylvias Press and serves on the poetry faculty at the Rainier Writing Workshop, a low-residency MFA program at Pacific Lutheran University. Agodon lives in Washington State on traditional lands of the Chimacum, Coast Salish, S'Klallam, and Suquamish people. Write to her at kelli@agodon.com or visit her website: www.agodon.com.

José A. Alcantara is a former construction worker, baker, commercial fisherman, math teacher, and studio photographer. His poems have appeared or are forthcoming in *Poetry Daily, The Southern Review, Spillway, Rattle,* and *Beloit Poetry Journal*, and have been shared on gratefulness.org.

Shari Altman grew up in the South but now lives in rural Vermont with her husband, three cats, eleven chickens, and several beehives. She is the cofounder of Literary North, a literary arts organization based in the Upper Valley of Vermont. Her work has been featured in *Amirisu, Taproot,* and *Bloodroot Literary Magazine.*

Born in New York City in 1950, **Julia Alvarez** has written ten novels, including *How the García Girls Lost Their Accents, In the Time of the Butterflies*, and *Afterlife*, as well as poetry collections, including *Homecoming, The Other Side/El Otro Lado*, and *The Woman I Kept to Myself.* Alvarez's awards include the Pura Belpré and Américas Awards for her books for young readers, the Hispanic Heritage Award, and the F. Scott Fitzgerald Award. In 2013, she received the National Medal of Arts from President Obama.

Ruth Arnison loves playing with words whether it be haiku, poetry, or short stories. She was the editor of Poems in the Waiting Room (NZ) for 13 years. She is the instigator of Lilliput Libraries—New

Zealand's little neighborhood libraries—and every summer paints poems on steps and seats around her hometown, Dunedin. In 2018 she was awarded the QSM (Queen's Service Medal) for services to poetry and literature.

Lahab Assef Al-Jundi was born and raised in Damascus, Syria. He attended The University of Texas at Austin, where he graduated with a degree in electrical engineering. Not long after graduation, he discovered his passion for writing and published his first poetry collection, *A Long Way*, in 1985. His latest poetry collection, *No Faith At All*, was published in 2014 by Pecan Grove Press. He lives in San Antonio, Texas.

David Axelrod's new collection of poems, *Years Beyond the River*, appeared in 2021 from Terrapin Books. His second collection of nonfiction, *The Eclipse I Call Father: Essays on Absence,* was published by Oregon State University Press in the spring of 2019. Axelrod directs the low-residency MFA and Wilderness, Ecology, and Community program at Eastern Oregon University. He makes his home in Missoula, Montana.

Zeina Azzam is a Palestinian American poet, editor, and community activist. Her chapbook, *Bayna Bayna, In-Between*, was released in 2021 by The Poetry Box. Zeina's poems are published or are forthcoming in *Pleiades, Passager, Gyroscope, Pensive Journal, Streetlight Magazine, Mizna, Sukoon Magazine, Barzakh, Making Levantine Cuisine, Tales from Six Feet Apart, Bettering American Poetry, Making Mirrors: Writing/Righting by and for Refugees, Gaza Unsilenced*, and others. She holds an MA in Arabic literature from Georgetown University.

Dave Baldwin retired from the Walt Disney Company (Technology Division) in 2017 after 40+ years as a technical writer and editor. In his career, he also worked for Boeing, Microsoft, Hewlett-Packard, and Amazon. He has been a naval officer, college teacher, and masters track and field athlete. In 2009, he served as the national secretary for the Haiku Society of America. Dave lives in Lake Stevens, Washington, a few miles north of Seattle.

Ellen Bass is a chancellor of the Academy of American Poets and author most recently of *Indigo* (Copper Canyon Press, 2020). Her book *Like a Beggar* (Copper Canyon Press, 2014) was a finalist for the Paterson Poetry Prize, the Publishing Triangle Award, the Milt Kessler Poetry Award, the Lambda Literary Award, and the Northern California Book Award. Previous books include *The Human Line* (Copper Canyon Press, 2007) and *Mules of Love* (BOA Editions, 2002).

Carolee Bennett is a writer and artist living in Upstate New York, where—after a local poetry competition—she has fun saying she's been the "almost" poet laureate of Smitty's Tavern. Her work has received recognition from Sundress Best of the Net, the Crab Creek Review Poetry Prize (semi-finalist), and the Tupelo Quarterly Poetry

Prize (finalist). She has an MFA in poetry from Ashland University and works full-time as a writer in social media marketing.

Kimberly Blaeser, former Wisconsin poet laureate, is the author of five poetry collections, including *Copper Yearning, Apprenticed to Justice,* and *Résister en dansant/Ikwe-niimi: Dancing Resistance.* An Anishinaabe activist and environmentalist from White Earth Reservation, Blaeser is a professor of English and Indigenous Studies at University of Wisconsin–Milwaukee, an MFA faculty member for the Institute of American Indian Arts in Santa Fe, and founding director of the literary organization In-Na-Po—Indigenous Nations Poets.

Sally Bliumis-Dunn's poems have appeared in *On the Seawall, Paris Review, Prairie Schooner, PLUME, Poetry London,* the *New York Times,* PBS NewsHour, *upstreet,* Poem-a-day, and Ted Kooser's column, among others. In 2018, her third book, *Echolocation* (Plume Editions/MadHat Press), was long-listed for the Julie Suk Award, runner-up for the Eric Hoffer Prize, and runner-up for the Poetry by the Sea Prize.

Chana Bloch was the author of several collections of poetry, including *The Secrets of the Tribe, The Past Keeps Changing, Mrs. Dumpty, Blood Honey,* and *Swimming in the Rain: New & Selected Poems* (Autumn House Press, 2015). She was cotranslator of the biblical *Song of Songs* as well as contemporary Israeli poetry. Her awards included the Poetry Society of America's Di Castagnola Award, the Felix Pollak Prize in Poetry, and the 2012 Meringoff Poetry Award.

Megan Buchanan is a teaching artist, a poet, a performer, a collaborative dancemaker, and an English teacher to students with language-based exceptionalities. Her collection *Clothesline Religion* (Green Writers Press, 2017) was nominated for the 2018 Vermont Book Award. Her work appears in numerous journals and anthologies, including *The Sun Magazine, make/shift,* and *A Woman's Thing.* She's grateful for support from the Arizona Commission on the Arts, Vermont Arts Council, Vermont Performance Lab, and the Vermont Studio Center. www.meganbuchanan.net

Dan Butler is known primarily as an actor whose credits include major roles on and off Broadway, on television, and in film, where he has also written, directed, and produced. In 2011, Dan adapted and directed a screen version of Poet Laureate Ted Kooser's verse poem "Pearl" starring Francis Sternhagen and himself, which had a great life on the film festival circuit. "New York Downpour" marks Dan's first published poem.

Kai Coggin is the author of *Mining for Stardust* (FlowerSong Press, 2021), *Incandescent* (Sibling Rivalry Press, 2019), *Wingspan* (Golden Dragonfly Press, 2016), and *Periscope Heart* (Swimming with Elephants Publications, 2014). She is a teaching artist in poetry with the Arkansas Arts Council, and the host of the longest-running consecutive weekly open mic series in the country, Wednesday Night Poetry. Her widely published poems have appeared in *Poetry, Cultural Weekly, SWWIM, Lavender Review*, and elsewhere.

Phyllis Cole-Dai began pecking away on an old manual typewriter in childhood and never stopped. She has authored or edited 11 books in multiple genres, "writing across what divides us." Her latest title is *Staying Power: Writings from a Pandemic Year* (Bell Sound Books, 2021). Originally from Ohio, she now resides with her scientist husband, college-bound son, and two cats in a 130-year-old house in Brookings, South Dakota. Learn more at phylliscoledai.com.

Karen Craigo is Missouri's fifth poet laureate, as well as the author of two books, *Passing Through Humansville* (Sundress, 2018) and *No More Milk* (Sundress, 2016). She is a freelance writer and editor and is based in Springfield, Missouri.

James Crews is the editor of the best-selling anthology *How to Love the World*, which has been featured on NPR's Morning Edition, in the *Boston Globe*, and the *Washington Post*, and is the author of four prize-winning collections of poetry: *The Book of What Stays, Telling My Father, Bluebird,* and *Every Waking Moment*. He lives with his husband in Shaftsbury, Vermont. jamescrews.net

Barbara Crooker is the author of nine books of poetry; *Some Glad Morning* (University of Pittsburgh, 2019) is the latest. Her honors include the WB Yeats Society of New York Award, the Thomas Merton Poetry of the Sacred Award, and three Pennsylvania Council on the Arts Fellowships. Her work appears in a variety of literary journals and anthologies, and has been read on ABC, the BBC, and The Writer's Almanac, and featured on Ted Kooser's American Life in Poetry.

An Officer of the Order of Canada, **Lorna Crozier** has been acknowledged for her contributions to Canadian literature with five honorary doctorates, most recently from McGill and Simon Fraser Universities. Her books have received numerous national awards, including the Governor-General's Award for Poetry. A professor emerita at the University of Victoria, she has performed for Queen Elizabeth II and has read her poetry, which has been translated into several languages, on every continent except Antarctica. Crozier lives on Vancouver Island.

Todd Davis is the author of seven books of poetry, most recently *Coffin Honey* (2022) and *Native Species* (2019), both published by Michigan State University Press. His writing has won the Foreword INDIES Book of the Year Bronze and Silver Awards, the Midwest Book Award, the Gwendolyn Brooks Poetry Prize, the Chautauqua Editors Prize, and the Bloomsburg University Book Prize. He teaches environmental studies at Pennsylvania State University's Altoona College.

Danny Dover is a retired piano technician living in Bethel, Vermont. He has two books of poetry: *Tasting Precious Metal* (published by Antrim House and available at norwichbookstore.com), and a chapbook, *Kindness Soup, Thankful Tea*. His poems have appeared in *Oberon, Himalayan Journal, Birchsong, Bloodroot,* and others, and also on two CDs of original music by Aaron Marcus of Montpelier, Vermont.

Kate Duignan is a New Zealand novelist and occasional poet. Her most recent novel, *The New Ships*, was short-listed in 2019 for the Acorn Prize, New Zealand's premier fiction prize. Kate is currently working on a collection of short stories. She teaches fiction at the IIML, Victoria University of Wellington. She lives in Wellington with her partner and children.

Cornelius Eady's poetry collections include *Victims of the Latest Dance Craze*, winner of the 1985 Lamont Prize; *The Gathering of My Name*, nominated for a 1992 Pulitzer Prize; and *Hardheaded Weather*. He teaches at the University of Tennessee, Knoxville and is cofounder of the Cave Canem Foundation.

Terri Kirby Erickson is the author of six collections, including *A Sun Inside My Chest* (Press 53). Her work has appeared in American Life in Poetry, *Atlanta Review, Healing the Divide: Poems of Kindness & Connection, How to Love the World: Poems of Gratitude and Hope, The Christian Century, The SUN,* on The Writer's Almanac, and many others. Her awards include the Joy Harjo Poetry Prize, the Atlanta Review International Publication Prize, and a Nautilus Silver Book Award. She lives in North Carolina.

Julia Fehrenbacher is a poet, a teacher, a life coach, and a sometimes-painter who is always looking for ways to spread a little good around in this world. She is most at home by the ocean and in the forests of the Pacific Northwest and with pen and paintbrush in hand. She lives in Corvallis, Oregon, with her husband and two beautiful girls.

Molly Fisk edited *California Fire & Water: A Climate Crisis Anthology,* with a Poets Laureate Fellowship from the Academy of American Poets when she was poet laureate of Nevada County, California. She's also won grants from the NEA, the California Arts Council, and the Corporation for Public Broadcasting. Her most recent poetry collection is *The More Difficult Beauty*; her latest book of radio commentary is *Naming Your Teeth*. Fisk lives in the Sierra foothills.
mollyfisk.com

Laura Foley is the author of seven poetry collections. *Why I Never Finished My Dissertation* received a starred Kirkus Review and an Eric Hoffer Award. Her collection *It's This* is forthcoming from Salmon Press. Her poems have won numerous awards and national recognition, been read by Garrison Keillor on The Writers' Almanac, and appeared in Ted Kooser's American Life in Poetry. Laura lives with her wife, Clara Gimenez, among Vermont hills.

Rebecca Foust is the author of three chapbooks and four books, including *Only*, forthcoming from Four Way Books in 2022, with poems in *The Hudson Review, Narrative, Ploughshares, Poetry, Southern Review,* and elsewhere. Recognitions include the 2020 Pablo Neruda Prize for Poetry, judged by Kaveh Akbar; the CP Cavafy and James Hearst poetry prizes; a Marin Poet Laureateship; and fellowships from The Frost Place, Hedgebrook, MacDowell, and Sewanee.

Rudy Francisco is one of the most recognizable names in spoken word poetry. He was born, raised, and still resides in San Diego, California. As an artist, Rudy Francisco is an amalgamation of social critique, introspection, honesty, and humor. He uses personal narratives to discuss the politics of race, class, gender, and religion while simultaneously pinpointing and reinforcing the interconnected nature of human existence. He is the author of *I'll Fly Away* (Button Poetry, 2020).

Joy Gaines-Friedler is the author of three books of poetry, including the award-winning *Capture Theory*. Joy teaches for nonprofits in the Detroit area, including Freedom House Detroit, where she offers the art of poetry to asylum seekers from western and northern Africa. She's also taught for the University of Michigan Prison Creative Arts Project (PCAP), where she worked with male lifers. Widely published, Joy has numerous awards and multiple Pushcart Prize nominations.

Ross Gay is the author of four books of poetry: *Against Which*; *Bringing the Shovel Down*; *Catalog of Unabashed Gratitude,* winner of the 2015 National Book Critics Circle Award and the 2016 Kingsley Tufts Poetry Award; and *Be Holding* (University of Pittsburgh Press, 2020).

His best-selling collection of essays, *The Book of Delights*, was released by Algonquin Books in 2019.

Alice Wolf Gilborn, a native of Colorado, is the founding editor of the literary magazine *Blueline,* published by the English department, SUNY Potsdam. Her poems have appeared in various journals and anthologies, most recently *Healing the Divide* (Green Writers Press) and *After Moby-Dick* (Spinner Publications). She is also author of a chapbook, *Taking Root* (Finishing Line Press), as well as a full-length book of poetry, *Apples and Stones* (Kelsay Books, 2020). alicewolfgilborn.com

Mary Ray Goehring, a snowbird, migrates between her central Wisconsin prairie and the pine forests of East Texas. She has been published in *Steam Ticket Review, Blue Heron Review, Ariel Anthology, Brick Street Poetry, Your Daily Poem, Texas Poetry Calendar, Bramble,* and several Wisconsin Fellowship of Poets poetry calendars. A retired landscape designer turned naturalist, she loves to write about family, friends, and nature.

Ingrid Goff-Maidoff is the author of more than a dozen books of poetry and inspiration, as well as a beautiful line of cards and gifts. Her books include *What Holds Us, Wild Song, Befriending the Soul, Good Mother Welcome,* and *Simple Graces for Every Meal.* She lives on the island of Martha's Vineyard with her husband and three white cats: Rumi, Hafiz, and Mirabai. Ingrid celebrates poetry, beauty, and spirit through her website, www.tendingjoy.com.

Nancy Gordon grew up in the Adirondacks, her true home, then taught English in New Jersey for years, including a year on exchange in New Zealand. A midlife marriage and move were followed by law school and years of law practice. She and her husband have returned home to the Adirondacks, and she now has more time for poetry, always an important part of her life.

Most recent of **David Graham's** seven collections of poetry is *The Honey of Earth* (Terrapin

Books, 2019). Others include *Stutter Monk* (Flume Press) and *Second Wind* (Texas Tech University Press). He coedited (with Tom Montag) the poetry anthology *Local News: Poetry About Small Towns* (MWPH Books, 2019) and with Kate Sontag the essay anthology *After Confession: Poetry as Confession* (Graywolf Press, 2001). He lives in Glens Falls, New York. www.davidgrahampoet.com

Leah Naomi Green is the author of *The More Extravagant Feast* (Graywolf Press, 2020), selected by Li-Young Lee for the Walt Whitman Award of the Academy of American Poets. She is the recipient of a 2021 Treehouse Climate Action Poetry Prize from the AAP, as well as the 2021 Lucille Clifton Legacy Award. Green teaches environmental studies and English at Washington and Lee University. Green lives in the mountains of Virginia, where she and her family homestead and grow food.

Twyla M. Hansen, Nebraska's state poet 2013–2018, codirects Poetry from the Plains, and conducts readings/workshops through Humanities Nebraska. Her book *Rock • Tree • Bird* won the 2018 WILLA Literary Award and Nebraska Book Award. Previous books won Nebraska Book Awards and a 2017 Notable Nebraska 150 Book. Recent publications: *Briar Cliff Review, Prairie Schooner, South Dakota Review, More in Time: A Tribute to Ted Kooser, Nebraska Poetry: A Sesquicentennial Anthology 1867–2017*, poets.org, poetryfoundation.org, poetryoutloud.org, and more.

Joy Harjo is an internationally renowned performer and writer of the Muscogee (Creek) Nation. She is serving her second term as the 23rd poet laureate of the United States. The author of nine books of poetry, including the highly acclaimed *An American Sunrise,* she has also written several plays and children's books, and two memoirs, *Crazy Brave* and *Poet Warrior.*

Penny Harter's most recent collections are *Still-Water Days* (2021) and *A Prayer the Body Makes* (2020). Her work has appeared in *Persimmon Tree, Rattle, Tiferet*, and American Life in Poetry, as well as in many journals, anthologies, and earlier collections. An invited reader at the 2010 Dodge Festival, she has won fellowships and awards from the New Jersey State Council on the Arts, VCCA, and the Poetry Society of America. For more information visit pennyharterpoet.com.

Margaret Hasse lives in Saint Paul, Minnesota, where she has been active as a teaching poet, among other work in the community. Six of Margaret's full-length poetry collections are in print. During the first year of the COVID-19 pandemic, Margaret collaborated with artist Sharon DeMark on *Shelter*, a collection of poems and paintings about refuge. A chapbook, *The Call of Glacier Park* (2022), is her latest publication. To learn more, visit her website: MargaretHasse.com.

Tom Hennen is the author of six books of poetry, including *Darkness Sticks to Everything: Collected and New Poems* (Copper Canyon Press, 2013), and was born and raised in rural Minnesota. After abandoning college, he married and began work as a letterpress and offset printer. He helped found the Minnesota Writer's Publishing House, then worked for the Department of Natural Resources wildlife section, and later at the Sand Lake National Wildlife Refuge in South Dakota. Now retired, he lives in Minnesota.

Zoe Higgins is a Pākehā poet and theatre-maker living in Te Whanganui-a-Tara in Aotearoa. Her work can be found in journals such as *Landfall, Sport, Starling*, and *Sweet Mammalian.*

Donna Hilbert's latest book is *Gravity: New & Selected Poems* (Tebot Bach, 2018). Her new collection, *Threnody*, is forthcoming from Moon Tide Press. She is a monthly contributing writer to the online journal *Verse-Virtual*. Her work has appeared in the

Los Angeles Times, Braided Way, Chiron Review, Sheila-Na-Gig, Rattle, Zocalo Public Square, One Art, and numerous anthologies. She writes and leads private workshops in Southern California, where she makes her home. Learn more at www.donnahilbert.com.

Jane Hirshfield's ninth, recently published poetry collection is *Ledger* (Knopf, 2020). A former chancellor of the Academy of American Poets, her work appears in *The New Yorker, The Atlantic, The Times Literary Supplement, The New York Review of Books,* and 10 editions of The Best American Poetry series. In 2019, she was elected to the American Academy of Arts and Sciences.

Linda Hogan is a Chickasaw poet, novelist, essayist, playwright, teacher, and activist who has spent most of her life in Oklahoma and Colorado. Her fiction has garnered many honors, including a Pulitzer Prize nomination, and her poetry collections have received the American Book Award, the Colorado Book Award, and a National Book Critics Circle nomination. Her latest book is *A History of Kindness* (Torrey House Press, 2020).

Marie Howe is the author of four books of poetry, the most recent of which is *Magdalene* (Norton). She was New York state poet from 2012 to 2014, is a chancellor of the Academy of American Poets, and teaches at Sarah Lawrence College. She is also the poet in residence at the Cathedral Church of Saint John the Divine in New York City.

After teaching public school in Alaska for about 30 years, **Ray Hudson** moved to Vermont. He is the author of *Moments Rightly Placed: An Aleutian Memoir*, along with several works on Aleutian history and ethnography. His most recent publication is a YA novel, *Ivory and Paper: Adventures In and Out of Time* (University of Alaska Press).

Mary Elder Jacobsen's poetry has appeared in *The Greensboro Review, Four Way Review, Green Mountains Review, storySouth, One,*

Poetry Daily, and anthologies, including *Healing the Divide: Poems of Kindness & Connection* (edited by James Crews). Winner of the Lyric Memorial Prize and recipient of a Vermont Studio Center residency, Jacobsen is co-organizer of Words Out Loud, an annual reading series of Vermont authors held at a still-unplugged 1823 meetinghouse.

Richard Jones's sixteen books include *Apropos of Nothing* (Copper Canyon, 2006), *The Correct Spelling & Exact Meaning* (Copper Canyon, 2010), and *Stranger on Earth* (Copper Canyon, 2018). He has two new books forthcoming, *Paris* and *Avalon*. For 40 years he has edited the literary journal *Poetry East* and curated its many anthologies, including *Origins, The Last Believer in Words,* and *Bliss*. He is professor of English at DePaul University in Chicago.

Fady Joudah is a Palestinian American physician, poet, and translator. He was born in Austin, Texas, but grew up in Libya and Saudi Arabia. Joudah's debut collection of poetry, *The Earth in the Attic* (2008), won the 2007 Yale Series of Younger Poets competition, chosen by Louise Glück. Joudah lives with his family in Houston, where he serves as a physician of internal medicine.

Jacqueline Jules is the author of *Manna in the Morning* (Kelsay Books, 2021), *Itzhak Perlman's Broken String* (Evening Street Press, 2017), *Field Trip to the Museum* (Finishing Line Press, 2014), and *Stronger Than Cleopatra* (ELJ Publications, 2014). She is also the author of 50 books for young readers, including the poetry collection *Tag Your Dreams: Poems of Play and Persistence* (Albert Whitman, 2020). Visit her online at www.jacquelinejules.com.

Christine Kitano is the author of two collections of poetry, *Birds of Paradise* (Lynx House Press) and *Sky Country* (BOA Editions), which won the Central New York Book Award and was a finalist for the Paterson Poetry Prize. She is coeditor of the forthcoming *They Rise Like a Wave* (Blue Oak Press), an anthology of

Asian American women and nonbinary poets. In addition to teaching at Ithaca College, she serves as Tompkins County poet laureate. christinekitano.com

Michael Kleber-Diggs is the author of *Worldly Things*, which was awarded the 2020 Max Ritvo Poetry Prize. He was born and raised in Kansas and now lives in St. Paul, Minnesota. His work has appeared in *Lit Hub, The Rumpus, Rain Taxi, McSweeney's Internet Tendency, Water~Stone Review, Midway Review,* and *North Dakota Quarterly*. Michael teaches poetry and creative nonfiction through the Minnesota Prison Writers Workshop.

Tricia Knoll lives in a Vermont woods. Her work appears widely in journals and anthologies, and has received nine Pushcart nominations and one Best of Net. Her collected poems include *Ocean's Laughter, Urban Wild, Broadfork Farm, How I Learned to Be White,* and *Checkered Mates. How I Learned to Be White* received the 2018 Indie Human Rights Award for Motivational Poetry. She is a contributing editor to *Verse-Virtual*. triciaknoll.com

The 13th US poet laureate (2004–2006), **Ted Kooser** is a retired life insurance executive who lives on acreage near the village of Garland, Nebraska, with his wife, Kathleen Rutledge. His collection *Delights & Shadows* was awarded the Pulitzer Prize in Poetry in 2005. His poems have appeared in *The Atlantic, The Hudson Review, The Antioch Review, The Kenyon Review,* and dozens of other literary journals. He is the author most recently of *Kindest Regards: New and Selected Poems* (2018) and *Red Stilts* (2020), both from Copper Canyon Press.

Danusha Laméris is the author of two books: *The Moons of August* (Autumn House, 2014), which was chosen by Naomi Shihab Nye as the winner of the Autumn House Press Poetry Prize, and *Bonfire Opera* (University of Pittsburgh, 2020), which won the Northern California

Book Award. Winner of the Lucille Clifton Legacy Award, she teaches in the Pacific University low-residency MFA program and cohosts with James Crews the Poetry of Resilience online seminars. She lives in Santa Cruz County, California.

Heather Lanier's memoir *Raising a Rare Girl* was a *New York Times Book Review* Editors' Choice. She is also the author of two award-winning poetry chapbooks. She is an assistant professor of creative writing at Rowan University, and her TED talk has been viewed over two million times. You can sign up for her newsletter, *The Slow Take*, by visiting her website, heatherlanierwriter.com.

Dorianne Laux's sixth collection, *Only as the Day Is Long: New and Selected Poems,* was named a finalist for the 2020 Pulitzer Prize for Poetry. Her fifth collection, *The Book of Men*, was awarded the Paterson Poetry Prize, and her fourth book of poems, *Facts About the Moon*, won the Oregon Book Award. Laux is the coauthor of the celebrated

The Poet's Companion: A Guide to the Pleasures of Writing Poetry.

Li-Young Lee was born in Djakarta, Indonesia, in 1957 to Chinese political exiles. He is the author of *The Undressing* (W. W. Norton, 2018); *Behind My Eyes* (W. W. Norton, 2008); *Book of My Nights* (BOA Editions, 2001), which won the 2002 William Carlos Williams Award; *The City in Which I Love You* (BOA Editions, 1990), which was the 1990 Lamont Poetry Selection; and *Rose* (BOA Editions, 1986), which won the Delmore Schwartz Memorial Poetry Award.

Paula Gordon Lepp lives in South Charleston, West Virginia, with her husband and two almost-grown kids. She grew up in a rural community in the Mississippi Delta, and a childhood spent roaming woods and fields, climbing trees, and playing in the dirt instilled in her a love for nature that is reflected in her poems. Paula's work has been published in the anthologies *How to Love the World:*

Poems of Gratitude and Hope and *The Mountain* (Middle Creek Publishing).

Annie Lighthart began writing poetry after her first visit to an Oregon old-growth forest and now teaches poetry wherever she can. Poems from her books *Iron String* and *Pax* have been featured on The Writer's Almanac and in many anthologies. Annie's work has been turned into music, been used in healing projects, and traveled farther than she has. She hopes you find a poem to love in this book, even if it is one she didn't write.

Ada Limón is the author of five poetry collections, including *The Carrying*, which won the National Book Critics Circle Award for Poetry. Her fourth book, *Bright Dead Things*, was named a finalist for the National Book Award, the Kingsley Tufts Poetry Award, and the National Book Critics Circle Award. A recipient of a Guggenheim Fellowship for Poetry, she serves on the faculty of the Queens University of Charlotte's low-residency MFA program and lives in Lexington, Kentucky.

Alison Luterman's four books of poetry are *The Largest Possible Life, See How We Almost Fly, Desire Zoo,* and *In the Time of Great Fires* (Catamaran Press, 2020). Her poems and stories have appeared in *The Sun, Rattle, Salon, Prairie Schooner, Nimrod, The Atlanta Review, Tattoo Highway*, and elsewhere. She has written an e-book of personal essays, *Feral City*; half a dozen plays; and a song cycle, as well as two musicals, *The Chain* and *The Shyest Witch*.

Emilie Lygren is a poet and an outdoor educator who holds a bachelor's degree in geology-biology from Brown University. Her poems have been published in *Thimble Literary Magazine, The English Leadership Quarterly, Solo Novo*, and several other literary journals. Her first book of poems, *What We Were Born For* (Blue Light Press, 2021), won the Blue Light Book Award. She lives in San Rafael, California.

Michelle Mandolia works as an analyst at the US Environmental Protection

Agency. She lives with her husband and two children in Reston, Virginia.

Joseph Millar is the author of six books of poetry, including *Dark Harvest: New and Selected Poems* (Carnegie Mellon University Press, 2021) and *Overtime* (Eastern Washington University Press, 2001), which was a finalist for the Oregon Book Award. He is the recipient of fellowships from the Guggenheim Foundation and the National Endowment for the Arts, and teaches in the MFA programs at North Carolina State and Pacific University.

Brad Aaron Modlin wrote *Everyone at This Party Has Two Names*, which won the Cowles Poetry Prize. *Surviving in Drought* (stories) won the Cupboard contest. His work has been the basis for orchestral scores, an art exhibition in New York City, and the premier episode of *Poetry Unbound* from On Being Studios. A professor and the Reynolds Endowed Chair of Creative Writing at the University of Nebraska at Kearney, he teaches

(under)graduates, coordinates the visiting writers' series, and gets chalk all over himself.

Susan Moorhead writes poetry and stories in New York. Her work has appeared in many journals and anthologies. She's received four Pushcart Prize nominations for fiction, nonfiction, and poetry, and first prize in the Greenburgh, New York, poetry contest. Her poetry collections are *The Night Ghost* and *Carry Darkness, Carry Light*. Daytimes find her working as a librarian, where she is happy to be surrounded by books.

Susan Musgrave lives on Haida Gwaii, a group of islands in the North Pacific that lie equidistant from Luxor, Machu Picchu, Ninevah, and Timbuktu. The high point of her literary career was finding her name in the index of *Montreal's Irish Mafia*. She has published more than 30 books and has received awards in six categories: poetry, novels, nonfiction, food writing, editing, and books for children. Her new book of poetry, *Exculpatory Lilies*, will be published by M&S in 2022.

With over a million copies sold, **Mark Nepo** has moved and inspired readers and seekers all over the world with his #1 *New York Times* bestseller *The Book of Awakening*. Beloved as a poet, teacher, and storyteller, Mark has been called "one of the finest spiritual guides of our time," "a consummate storyteller," and "an eloquent spiritual teacher." A best-selling author, he has published 22 books and recorded 14 audio projects. Recent work includes *The Book of Soul* (St. Martin's Essentials, 2020) and *Drinking from the River of Light* (Sounds True, 2019), a Nautilus Award winner. marknepo.com and threeintentions.com

Suzanne Nussey has worked as an editor, writer, memoir coach, and writing instructor in Ottawa, Canada. Her poetry, creative nonfiction, and essays have been published in *The New Quarterly, EVENT, The Fiddlehead, Prairie Fire*, and *Spark and Echo*, among others, and have won several national Canadian literary competitions. Suzanne has also developed and facilitated creative writing workshops for women living in shelters. She holds master's degrees in creative writing (Syracuse University) and pastoral counseling (St. Paul University).

Naomi Shihab Nye is the Young People's Poet Laureate of the United States (Poetry Foundation). Her most recent books are *Everything Comes Next, Collected & New Poems, Cast Away: Poems for Our Time* (poems about trash), *The Tiny Journalist,* and *Voices in the Air: Poems for Listeners*. She lives in San Antonio, Texas.

January Gill O'Neil is an associate professor of English at Salem State University. She is the author of *Rewilding* (CavanKerry Press, 2018), a finalist for the 2019 Paterson Poetry Prize; *Misery Islands* (CavanKerry Press, 2014); and *Underlife* (CavanKerry Press, 2009).

Gregory Orr is the author of two books about poetry, *Poetry as Survival* and *A Primer for Poets and Readers of Poetry*; a memoir, *The Blessing*; and 12 collections of poetry, including *How Beautiful the Beloved* and *The Last Love Poem I Will Ever Write*. He taught at the University of Virginia from 1975 to 2019, where he founded the university's MFA program in creative writing.

Alicia Ostriker is professor emerita of English at Rutgers University and a faculty member of Drew University's low-residency poetry MFA program. In 2018, she was named New York state poet by Governor Andrew Cuomo. Ostriker served as chancellor of the Academy of American Poets from 2015 to 2021. She lives in New York City.

Peter Pereira is a family physician in Seattle whose poems have appeared in *Poetry, Prairie Schooner, New England Review, Virginia Quarterly Review,* and *Journal of the American Medical Association.* His books include *What's Written*

on the Body (Copper Canyon Press, 2007), which was a finalist for the Washington State Book Award; *Saying the World* (Copper Canyon Press, 2003), which won the 2002 Hayden Carruth Award; and the limited-edition chapbook *The Lost Twin* (Grey Spider Press, 2000).

Andrea Potos is the author of several poetry collections, including *Marrow of Summer* (Kelsay Books), *Mothershell* (Kelsay Books), and *Yaya's Cloth* (Iris Press). Her poems most recently appeared in *Spirituality & Health Magazine, Poetry East, The Sun, Braided Way,* and *How to Love the World: Poems of Gratitude and Hope.* Andrea lives in Madison, Wisconsin.

Susan Rich is an award-winning poet, editor, and essayist. She is the author of *Cloud Pharmacy, The Alchemist's Kitchen, Cures Include Travel,* and *The Cartographer's Tongue.* She coedited the anthology *The Strangest of Theatres* (McSweeney's Books) and has received awards from PEN America and the Fulbright

Foundation. *Gallery of Postcards and Maps: New and Collected Poems* is forthcoming from Salmon Press, and *Blue Atlas* from Red Hen Press in 2024.

Jack Ridl, poet laureate of Douglas, Michigan, recently released *Saint Peter and the Goldfinch* (Wayne State University Press). His *Practicing to Walk Like a Heron* (WSU Press, 2013) was awarded the National Gold Medal for poetry by ForeWord Reviews/Indie Fab. His collection *Broken Symmetry* (WSU Press) was corecipient of the Society of Midland Authors Best Book of Poetry Award for 2006. For more information about Jack, visit: www.ridl.com.

Alberto Ríos was named Arizona's first poet laureate in 2013. He is the author of many poetry collections from Copper Canyon Press, including *Not Go Away Is My Name* (2020); *A Small Story About the Sky* (2015); *The Dangerous Shirt* (2009); *The Theater of Night* (2006); and *The Smallest Muscle in the Human Body* (2002), which was nominated for the National Book Award.

David Romtvedt is a writer and musician from Buffalo, Wyoming. His books include *Dilemmas of the Angels; Some Church;* the novel *Zelestina Urza in Outer Space*; and *The Tree of Gernika*, translations of the nineteenth-century Basque poet Joxe Mari Iparragirre. A recipient of the Pushcart Prize and of fellowships from the Wyoming Arts Council and the National Endowment for the Arts, Romtvedt also performs older and more contemporary Basque dance music with the band Ospa.

Susan Rothbard's poems have appeared in *Paterson Literary Review, The Comstock Review, English Journal, Dogwood,* and *Spindrift*. She earned her MFA in creative writing at Fairleigh Dickinson University, and her recent book, *Birds of New Jersey* (Broadkill River Press), was awarded the Dogfish Head Poetry Prize.

Ellen Rowland creates, concocts, and forages when she's not writing. She is the author of *Light Come Gather Me,* a selection of mindfulness haiku, and *Everything I Thought I Knew*, a collection of essays about living, learning, and parenting outside the status quo. Her writing has appeared in various literary journals and in several poetry anthologies. She lives off the grid on a tiny island in Greece. Connect with her at ellenrowland.com.

Patricia McKernon Runkle values the quiet work of listening to one another and building community. She has volunteered at a peer-support center for grieving children and their families, worked as a writer and editor, and directed a choir. She has published poems, songs and collaborative choral pieces, and an award-winning memoir on grief. She and her husband cherish their two grown children. griefscompass.com

Marjorie Saiser's seventh collection, *Learning to Swim* (Stephen F. Austin State University Press, 2019), contains both poetry and memoir. Her novel-in-poems, *Losing the Ring in the River* (University of New Mexico Press), won the WILLA Award for Poetry in 2014. Saiser's most recent book, *The Track the Whales Make: New & Selected Poems,* is available from University of Nebraska Press. Her website is www.poetmarge.com.

Lailah Dainin Shima walks and writes on the shores of Lake Wingra. She loves folding poems into envelopes she drops into mailboxes and forgets. Some of them have shown up in *One Art Poetry, Buddhist Poetry Review*, and *CALYX Journal.*

Faith Shearin is the author of six books of poetry: *The Owl Question, The Empty House, Moving the Piano, Telling the Bees, Orpheus Turning,* and *Lost Language*. Recent work has appeared in *Alaska Quarterly Review* and *Poetry East*, and has been read aloud by Garrison Keillor on The Writers' Almanac.

Michael Simms is an American poet and literary publisher. His most recent books are

American Ash and *Nightjar*. His poems have been published in literary journals and magazines, including *5 A.M., Poetry, Black Warrior Review, Mid-American Review, Pittsburgh Quarterly, Southwest Review*, and *West Branch*. He is the founder and editor of *Vox Populi*.

Anya Silver (1968–2018) won a Guggenheim Fellowship and the Georgia Author of the Year Award. She was the author of five books of poetry: *The Ninety-Third Name of God* (2010), *I Watched You Disappear* (2014), *From Nothing* (2016), and *Saint Agnostica* (2021), all published by the Louisiana State University Press, as well as *Second Bloom*, which was published in 2017 by Cascade Books. Until her death, she taught English at Mercer University in Macon, Georgia.

Tracy K. Smith is the author of the memoir *Ordinary Light* and four books of poetry: *Wade in the Water* (2018); *Life on Mars*, which received the 2012 Pulitzer Prize; *Duende*, recipient of the 2006 James Laughlin Award; and

The Body's Question, which won the 2002 Cave Canem Poetry Prize. In 2017 she was named the 22nd US poet laureate by the Library of Congress, 2017–2019.

Judith Sornberger is the author of four poetry collections: *Angel Chimes: Poems of Advent and Christmas* (Shanti Arts), *I Call to You from Time* (Wipf and Stock), *Practicing the World* (CavanKerry), and *Open Heart* (Calyx Books). Her prose memoir, *The Accidental Pilgrim: Finding God and His Mother in Tuscany*, is published by Shanti Arts. She is professor emerita of Mansfield University, where she taught English and women's studies. She lives on the side of a mountain in the northern Appalachians of Pennsylvania.

Kim Stafford directs the Northwest Writing Institute at Lewis & Clark College, and is the author of a dozen books, including *The Muses Among Us: Eloquent Listening and Other Pleasures of the Writer's Craft* (University of Georgia Press, 2003) and *Singer Come from Afar* (Red Hen Press,

2021). He has taught writing in Scotland, Mexico, Italy, and Bhutan. He served as Oregon poet laureate, 2018–2020. He teaches and travels to raise the human spirit.

William Stafford's (1914–1993) first collection of poems, *West of Your City*, wasn't published until he was in his mid-forties. However, by the time of his death, Stafford had published hundreds of poems, and was said to have written at least one new poem a day. His collection *Traveling Through the Dark* won the National Book Award for Poetry in 1963. Stafford also received the Award in Literature from the American Academy and Institute of Arts and Letters and a National Endowment for the Arts Senior Fellowship.

Julie Cadwallader Staub grew up with five sisters beside one of Minnesota's lakes. Her favorite words to hear were "Now you girls go outside and play." She now lives and writes from her home near Burlington, Vermont. Her poems have been published in literary journals and anthologies, including in *Poetry of*

Presence: An Anthology of Mindfulness Poems. Her two collections of poems are *Face to Face* (Cascadia Publishing, 2010) and *Wing Over Wing* (Paraclete Press, 2019).

Christine Stewart-Nuñez, South Dakota's poet laureate, is the author of seven books of poetry, most recently *The Poet & The Architect, Untrussed,* and *Bluewords Greening*, winner of the 2018 Whirling Prize. She's also the founder of the Women Poets Collective, a regional group focused on advancing its members' writing through peer critique and support.

Jacqueline Suskin is a poet and educator based in Northern California, where she is currently the artist in residence at Folklife Farm. Suskin is the author of seven books, including *Every Day Is a Poem* (Sounds True, 2020) and *Help in the Dark Season* (Write Bloody, 2019). With her project Poem Store, Suskin has composed over 40,000 improvisational poems for patrons who chose a topic in exchange for a unique verse. She was honored by Michelle Obama as a Turnaround Artist, and her work has been featured in the *New York Times,* the *Los Angeles Times, The Atlantic*, and other publications. For more, see jacquelinesuskin.com.

Joyce Sutphen grew up on a small farm in Stearns County, Minnesota. Her first collection of poems, *Straight Out of View*, won the Barnard New Women Poets Prize; her recent books are *The Green House* (Salmon Poetry, 2017) and *Carrying Water to the Field: New and Selected Poems* (University of Nebraska Press, 2019). She is the Minnesota poet laureate and professor emerita of literature and creative writing at Gustavus Adolphus College.

Heather Swan's poems have appeared in such journals as *Terrain, The Hopper, Poet Lore, Phoebe,* and *The Raleigh Review*, and her book of poems, *A Kinship with Ash* (Terrapin Books), was published in 2020. Her non-fiction has appeared in *Aeon, Belt, Catapult, Emergence, ISLE,* and *Terrain*. Her book *Where Honeybees Thrive:*

Stories from the Field (Penn State Press) won the Sigurd F. Olson Nature Writing Award. She teaches environmental literature and writing at the University of Wisconsin–Madison.

Angela Narciso Torres is the author of *Blood Orange*, winner of the Willow Books Literature Award for Poetry. Her recent collections include *To the Bone* (Sundress, 2020) and *What Happens Is Neither* (Four Way Books, 2021). Her work has appeared in *Poetry, Missouri Review, Quarterly West, Cortland Review*, and *PANK*. Born in Brooklyn and raised in Manila, she serves as a senior and reviews editor for *RHINO Poetry*.

Natasha Trethewey's first collection of poetry, *Domestic Work* (Graywolf Press, 2000), was selected by Rita Dove as the winner of the inaugural Cave Canem Poetry Prize. She is also the author of *Monument: Poems New and Selected* (Houghton Mifflin, 2018). In 2012, Trethewey was named both the State Poet Laureate of Mississippi and the 19th US poet laureate by the Library of Congress. Trethewey is the Board of Trustees Professor of English at Northwestern University in Evanston, Illinois.

Rosemerry Wahtola Trommer lives on the banks of the San Miguel River in southwest Colorado. She cohosts the *Emerging Form* podcast, the Stubborn Praise poetry series, and Secret Agents of Change (a kindness cabal). Her poems have been featured on A Prairie Home Companion, American Life in Poetry, and PBS News Hour, and in *Oprah Magazine*. Her most recent book, *Hush*, won the Halcyon Prize. One-word mantra: Adjust.

A retired educator of young children, **David Van Houten** moved from Michigan to Tucson, Arizona, with his husband in 2010. His interest in writing was cultivated by instructor Dan Gilmore at the Osher Lifelong Learning Institute at the University of Arizona. David is a docent at the University of Arizona Poetry Center and participates in their "Free Time" workshop, corresponding with writers who are incarcerated. David's poems were published in the *Oasis Journal* in 2017.

Connie Wanek was born in Wisconsin, was raised in New Mexico, and lived for over a quarter century in Duluth, Minnesota. She is the author of *Bonfire* (New Rivers Press), winner of the New Voices Award; *Hartley Field* (Holy Cow! Press); and *On Speaking Terms* (Copper Canyon Press). In 2016, the University of Nebraska Press published Wanek's *Rival Gardens: New and Selected Poems* as part of their Ted Kooser Contemporary Poetry series.

Gillian Wegener lives in central California. She is the author of *The Opposite of Clairvoyance* (2008) and *This Sweet Haphazard* (2017), both from Sixteen Rivers Press. She is the founding president of Modesto-Stanislaus Poetry Center, a past poet laureate for the City of Modesto and, as a volunteer, taught creative writing to teens in juvenile detention for five years.

Laura Grace Weldon has published three poetry collections—*Portals* (Middle Creek,

2021), *Blackbird* (Grayson, 2019), and *Tending* (Aldrich, 2013)—as well as a handbook of alternative education titled *Free Range Learning* (Hohm Press, 2010). She served as Ohio Poet of the Year and recently won the Halcyon Poetry Prize. She works as a book editor, teaches writing workshops, and maxes out her library card each week. Connect with her on Twitter, Facebook, and at lauragraceweldon.com.

Michelle Wiegers is a poet and mind-body life coach based in southern Vermont. Her work has appeared in *Healing the Divide, How to Love the World, Birchsong Anthology,* and *Third Wednesday*, among other journals. In her coaching work, she is a passionate advocate for those who suffer with chronic pain and fatigue. michellewiegers.com

Laura Budofsky Wisniewski is the author of the collection *Sanctuary, Vermont* (Orison Books) and the chapbook *How to Prepare Bear* (Redbird Chapbooks). Her work has appeared in *Image, Hunger Mountain Review, American*

Journal of Poetry, Passengers Journal, Confrontation, and others. She is winner of the 2020 Orison Poetry Prize, *Ruminate Magazine*'s 2020 Janet B. McCabe Poetry Prize, the 2019 Poetry International Prize, and the 2014 Passager Poetry Prize. Laura lives in a small town in Vermont.

Susan Zimmerman is a retired lawyer who lives and writes in Toronto. Her poetry chapbook, *Nothing Is Lost*, was published by Caitlin Press, and her poems are published in periodicals such as *Room, Fiddlehead, The Ontario Review, Fireweed, Matrix,* and *Calyx*. She has taught a creative writing course called Writing like Breathing at a healing center, and since her retirement in 2015, she has returned to participating regularly in poetry retreats and workshops.

CREDITS

"Praise" by Kelli Russell Agodon originally published in *Redivider*.

"Hot Tea" by Lahab Assef Al-Jundi originally published in *KNOT Literary Magazine* and *San Antonio Express-News*.

"Vain Doubts" and "Love Portions" Copyright © 2004 by Julia Alvarez. From *The Woman I Kept to Myself*, published by Algonquin Books of Chapel Hill. By permission of Susan Bergholz Literary Services, New York, NY, and Lamy, NM. All rights reserved.

"The Innermost Chamber of My Home Is Yours" by David Axelrod from *Years Beyond the River* Copyright © 2021 David Axelrod. Reprinted with permission of Terrapin Books.

"My Father's Hands" by Zeina Azzam, originally published in *Heartwood Literary Magazine* (2017) and in *Bayna Bayna, In-Between* (The Poetry Box) © 2021 by Zeina Azzam. Reprinted with permission of the author.

Ellen Bass, "The Thing Is" from *Mules of Love*. Copyright © 2002 by Ellen Bass. Reprinted with the permission of The Permissions Company, LLC on behalf of BOA Editions Ltd., boaeditions.org.

"Exactly 299,792,458 Meters Per Second" by Carolee Bennett originally published in *Contrary Magazine* (2017) and *Sundress Best of the Net Anthology* (2018).

"About Standing (in Kinship)" by Kimberly Blaeser originally published in *Poetry Magazine* (March 2021).

"Mailman" by Sally Bliumis-Dunn from *Second Skin* (Wind Publications, 2010). Reprinted with permission of the author.

"The Joins" by Chana Bloch from *Swimming in the Rain: New & Selected Poems* (Autumn House Press, 2015). Copyright © 2015 by Chana Bloch. Reprinted with permission of the publisher.

"Into Wildflower Into Field" by Kai Coggin from *Mining for Stardust* (FlowerSong Press, 2021). Reprinted with permission of the author.

"Ladder" by Phyllis Cole-Dai from *Staying Power: Writings from a Pandemic Year* (Bell Sound Books, 2021). Reprinted with permission of the author.

"Last Scraps of Color in Missouri" by Karen Craigo originally published in *The New York Times*. Reprinted with permission of the author.

"Self-Compassion" by James Crews originally appeared as part of the Academy of American Poets Poem-a-Day, edited by Kimberly Blaeser. "The Pool" by James Crews from *Every Waking Moment* (Lynx House Press, 2021). James Crews, "Self-Care," originally appeared in One Art edited by Mark Danowsky.

"Sustenance" by Barbara Crooker from *Small Rain* (Purple Flag, 2014), and "Forsythia" in *More In Time: A Tribute to Ted Kooser* (University of Nebraska Press, 2021). Reprinted with permission of the author.

"Heliotropic" by Todd Davis from *In the Kingdom of the Ditch* Copyright © 2013 Todd Davis (Michigan State University Press, 2013). Reprinted with permission of the author.

"Grandmother" by Kate Duignan originally published in *Sport 36, New Zealand New Writing*, Winter 2008, Victoria University Press, Wellington, NZ.

"A Small Moment" by Cornelius Eady from *Hardheaded Weather: New & Selected Poems* (Putnam, 2008). Reprinted with permission of the author.

"Free Breakfast" by Terri Kirby Erickson from *A Sun Inside My Chest* (Press 53, 2020). Reprinted by permission of the author and the publisher. "Night Talks" originally published in *ONE ART: a journal of poetry* (2020).

"Before I gained all this weight" by Molly Fisk originally published in *Cultural Weekly* and *Stone Gathering*, edited by Deborah Jacobs.

"A Perfect Arc" by Laura Foley from *Syringa*. © StarMeadow Press, 2007. Reprinted with permission. "Learning by Heart" from *Panoply Zine*.

"Kinship of Flesh" by Rebecca Foust from *Mom's Canoe* (Texas Review Press, 2009).

"Mercy" by Rudy Francisco from *Helium*. Copyright © 2017 by Rudy Francisco. Courtesy of Button Publishing Inc.

Ross Gay, "Thank You" from *Against Which*. Copyright © 2006 by Ross Gay. Reprinted with the permission of The Permissions Company, LLC on behalf of CavanKerry Press, Ltd., cavankerrypress.org.

"Wake Up" by Alice Gilborn from *Apples & Stones* (Kelsay Books, 2020). Reprinted with permission of the author.

"Peace Came Today" by Ingrid Goff-Maidoff from *Wild Song* (Sarah's Circle, 2021). Reprinted with permission of the author.

"The Age of Affection" by Leah Naomi Green, forthcoming in *Orion Magazine*.

"Trying to Pray" by Twyla M. Hansen from *Rock • Tree • Bird* (Backwaters Press, 2017). Reprinted with permission of the author.

"For Keeps," from *Conflict Resolution for Holy Beings: Poems* by Joy Harjo. Copyright © 2015 by Joy Harjo. Used by permission of W. W. Norton & Company, Inc.

"Two Meteors" by Penny Harter from *A Prayer the Body Makes* (Kelsay Books, 2020). Reprinted with permission of the author.

"Clothing" by Margaret Hasse from *Shelter* (Nodin Press, 2020). Reprinted with permission of author and publisher.

Tom Hennen, "Made Visible" from *Darkness Sticks to Everything: Collected and New Poems*. Copyright © 1997 by Tom Hennen. Reprinted with the permission of The Permissions Company, LLC on behalf of Copper Canyon Press, coppercanyonpress.org.

"Ode" by Zoe Higgins originally published in *Poems in the Waiting Room* (NZ), edited by Ruth Arnison.

"Credo" by Donna Hilbert from *Gravity: New & Selected Poems* (Tebot Bach, 2018). Reprinted with permission of the author.

"Arctic Night, Lights Across the Sky" by Linda Hogan from *A History of Kindness* (Torrey House Press, 2020). Reprinted with permission of the publisher.

"Delivery" by Marie Howe Copyright © 2017 by Marie Howe.

"Sponge Bath" by Mary Elder Jacobsen is part I of a two-part poem first published in *storySouth*. Copyright

"In Praise of Dirty Socks" by Lailah Dainin Shima, originally published in *The Buddhist Poetry Review.*

"Late Summer" by Anya Silver from *Second Bloom* (Cascade Books, 2017). Used by permission of Wipf and Stock Publishers, www.wipfandstock.com.

"The Summer You Learned to Swim" by Michael Simms originally published in *Poetry* (March 2021).

Tracy K. Smith, "Song" from *Life on Mars*. Copyright © 2011 by Tracy K. Smith. Reprinted with the permission of The Permissions Company, LLC on behalf of Graywolf Press, Minneapolis, MN, graywolfpress.org.

"Assisted Living" by Judith Sornberger originally published in *Third Wednesday.*

William Stafford, "You Reading This, Be Ready" from *Ask Me: 100 Essential Poems.* Copyright © 1977, 2014 by William Stafford and the Estate of William Stafford. Reprinted with the permission of The Permissions Company, LLC on behalf of Graywolf Press, Minneapolis, MN, graywolfpress.org.

"Turning" from *Wing Over Wing* by Julie Cadwallader Staub Copyright © 2019 by Julie Cadwallader Staub. Used by permission of Paraclete Press, www.paracletepress.com.

"Site Planning" by Christine Stewart-Nuñez from *The Poet & the Architect* Copyright © 2021 Christine Stewart-Nuñez. Reprinted with permission of Terrapin Books.

"Future" by Jacqueline Suskin from *Help in the Dark Season* (Write Bloody, 2019). Reprinted with permission of the author.

"Carrying Water to the Field" by Joyce Sutphen from *Carrying Water to the Field: New and Selected Poems* (University of Nebraska Press, 2019). Reprinted with permission of the author.

"On Lightness" and "Bowl" by Heather Swan from *A Kinship with Ash*. Copyright © 2020 Heather Swan. Reprinted with permission of Terrapin Books.

"Chore" by Angela Narciso Torres from *What Happens Is Neither*. Copyright © 2021 by Angela Narciso Torres. Reprinted with the permission of The Permissions Company, LLC, on behalf of Four Way Books, fourwaybooks.com.

Natasha Trethewey, "Housekeeping" from *Domestic Work*. Copyright © 2000 by Natasha Trethewey. Reprinted with the permission of The Permissions Company, LLC on behalf of Graywolf Press, graywolfpress.org.

"Kindness" and "The Question" by Rosemerry Wahtola Trommer, originally published on her blog, A Hundred Falling Veils.

"Breathe" by David Van Houten from *2020 Visions* (2021).

"Most Important Word" and "Thursday Morning" by Laura Grace Weldon from *Portals* (Middlecreek Publishing, 2021). Reprinted with permission of the author.

"Moving" by Michelle Wiegers originally published as part of The Gatherings Project.

"A Beginner's Guide to Gardening Alone" by Laura Budofsky Wisniewski first appeared in the 2020 *Mizmor Anthology* as "Suddenly While Gardening," and is forthcoming in *Sanctuary, Vermont* (Orison Books, 2022). Reprinted with permission of the author.

All other poems reprinted with permission of the author.

ACKNOWLEDGMENTS

My deepest thanks to the amazing team at Storey Publishing, who once again brought such a beautiful book into being, especially Deborah Balmuth, Liz Bevilacqua, Alethea Morrison, Alee Moncy, Jennifer Travis, and Melinda Slaving. I'm grateful for the community of poets who contributed to this book, too, some of whom I first met in Zoom workshops: These anthologies would not be possible without your generosity. Special thanks to my mentors and friends, especially Ted Kooser and Naomi Shihab Nye: You are both my North Stars in poetry as well as in life. Deepest appreciation to Danusha Laméris for her generous and beautiful foreword, and for the anchor of her timeless poems: I can't believe we get to be coworkers. Thank you to my family and friends, and to all the poetry readers out there (you are the best). Thanks to Dinara Mirtalipova for another gorgeous cover and for her own beautiful work. I couldn't do any of this without the essential support of my husband and best friend, Brad Peacock, who has taught me more about kindness than I ever thought possible, and who still asks me, when I need to hear it: "Are you happy to be alive?"